P9-DND-693

People with Dirty Hands

People with Dirty Hands

The Passion for Gardening

Robin Chotzinoff

Macmillan • USA

MACMILLAN
A Simon & Schuster Macmillan Company
1633 Broadway
New York, NY 10019

Copyright © 1996 by Robin Chotzinoff

All rights reserved. No part of this book may be reproduced or transmitted
in any form by any means, electronic or mechanical, including photo-
copying, recording, or by any other information storage and retrieval
system, without permission from the Publisher.

MACMILLAN is a registered trademark of Macmillan, Inc.

Library of Congress Cataloging-in-Publication Data

Chotzinoff, Robin.

People with dirty hands : the passion for gardening / Robin Chotzinoff.

p.   cm.
ISBN 0-02-860990-5 (hc)
1. Gardening—United States—Anecdotes.
2. Gardeners—United States—Anecdotes.
3. Chotzinoff, Robin.   I. Title.
SB455.C48   1996
635'.092'2—dc20
[B]   95-30585
CIP

Manufactured in the United States of America

10 9 8 7 6 5

Book Design by C&T Designs

This book is for Patty Calhoun,

because she gave me work.

Contents

*I*ntroduction

*I have grown further and further from my muse, and
closer and closer to my post-hole digger.*

E. B. WHITE

Zelma Stunkard became my next-door neighbor
eleven years ago. Her yard was clearly visible through the strands of old
wire fence that separated our properties. I saw Zelma and her boyfriend,
Vern Wiley, slogging through the spring mud. Zelma was seventy-six
then—she is eighty-six now—and she moved through the garden in a
plaid western snap shirt, double-knit stretch pants, and pink curlers.
Sometimes she wore an apron. She was usually followed by two medium-
mutt dogs and drifts of cats.

Vern was partial to a western look, too. He wore a tractor cap and
spit tobacco juice in a coffee can he carried around for that purpose.
All that spring, I heard Zelma and Vern disagreeing about anything that
could possibly happen in a garden. Zelma did not hold with straight lines
and planting in rows. She liked things wild. Vern said this approach made
weeding impossible, and implied it was an unnecessary expression of self.
Zelma implied right back at him that weeding, in itself, was unnecessary. She liked to give weeds a stay of execution. Sometimes, she pointed
out, they turned out to be violets or columbines. When Vern went
after the snowball tree with his pruning saw, Zelma said nothing, but
from the look on her face you would have thought he was sawing off
her fingers one by one. Vern was always reading up on the wonderful
new technologies. You could plant tomatoes in truck tires, he said. You
could make a compost spinner out of a forty-gallon oil can. Zelma did
not like technology in her garden. It made me wonder how two people
can possibly coexist in one garden.

"They can't," Zelma said bluntly. "This is my garden. Vern is my boyfriend and he's living here, but I own all this. You notice I don't marry him."

By then, I knew Zelma well enough to know that she came to the eastern Colorado plains in the early 1920s walking alongside a covered wagon, her nose stuck in a book and her hand on the wagon rail so she didn't veer off the path. She and her first husband worked on a remote ranch in the mountains—he as a cowboy, she as a cook. Their eight-year-old son drowned there, in an overloaded creek, and grief drove them into the city. For years, Zelma worked as a bookkeeper.

Her further work, though, was her garden. Clarence, her husband, stayed out of it, expressing his creative side in elaborate Christmas decorations. When Clarence died, Zelma married his friend, a plains rancher named Leith Stunkard. Leith had what Zelma called "a nice house in Sterling where you have to keep your yard just so." Zelma, who was constitutionally incapable of gardening "just so," kept her Denver house and garden as a sort of refuge, and when Leith died seven years later, she came back.

After a decent period of mourning, Zelma went to the local senior center tea dance and came back with Vern. He helped out around the place and gave her someone to argue with.

The yard they worked in together, cantankerously, was beautiful. Out of the mud grew columbines, roses, purple beans that turn green when you cook them, heads of lettuce, towers of tomatoes. There was a wooden picnic table under the grape arbor, where Zelma sat all day when she wasn't actively gardening. She shelled peas, wrote letters, and mended clothes there. The older she got, she said, the less she wanted to be inside. She never tired of outside chores—picking the sweet corn, cutting a bouquet of flowers, sprinkling the lawn by hand. Inside chores, such as baking seven pies for Thanksgiving, struck her as numbing. At the height of summer, Zelma moved herself from the grape arbor to an old Ford bench seat stationed on her front porch.

I moved away from Zelma and my old neighborhood seven years ago, but her yard is still my working definition of heaven. Following Zelma's model, I got into the habit not just of growing things, but of doing it idiosyncratically. Following Zelma's model, I will age ungracefully until I become an old woman in a small garden, doing whatever the hell I want. There was a time when this would have sounded unfulfilled to me, if not downright depressing, but now I look forward to it.

Because of Zelma, no matter where I go, I will always grow something, even if the prospect is daunting. As I write this, I am preparing to move to a north-facing mountain cabin with a sixty-five-day growing season. But so what? As a gardener, I have all the time in the world. Sooner or later, I will find out what thrives way up there, and cultivate it.

It was Zelma who got me into the habit of talking to gardeners. I like to write portraits of people, but given the choice, I prefer to write about gardeners. They are much more interesting than real people. In writing this book, I spent a year chewing over such subjects as the hotness of chile, the sweetness of old roses, the curative powers of wax myrtle, and over and over again, the benefits of being an old woman in a garden. All the gardeners I met were generous. They gave me plants, seeds, phone numbers, food, and advice—and not always about gardening, either. They were (almost) all as informal as I am, or more so. During this year of the people with dirty hands, I was not obliged to buy a single pair of pantyhose. And they all had their particular magnificent obsessions, which I love.

Why? If I knew, I would know why the wiry daisies on the east side of my house are coming up again, even though they have been sat on all winter, first by three feet of snow and then by a smelly black dog that wandered in and made this his bed. I don't know how it works, but the daisies are up again. How wonderful.

1 Rustling Roses

The old roses have recently wriggled
their way back into favor, and small
wonder. They give so little trouble
for so great a reward.

VITA SACKVILLE-WEST

It's very, very hot. The metal clippers in my hip pocket burn the rivets in my jeans. On my first day as a rose rustler, I have landed outside the gates of a hundred-year-old Jewish cemetery. I have done my share of time in graveyards, but never before have I come across one gated and locked at high noon.

Looking through the fence, I wonder if this is the wrong place to start. The graves are too well tended, and even now lawnmowers hum through the grass, cutting down the wild plants I seek. But I start out anyway, holding my cooler and my Ziploc bags and hugging the property line. I walk all around the perimeter without finding an opening. Finally, I pull up level with the grounds crew and shout through the fence.

"You got any roses in there?"

The two grounds guys are young and hip, jeans hanging down beyond the white rim of their underpants. They wipe the sweat off their faces, and one of them gives me a look reserved for middle-aged women who gather flora.

"We got a few," he says. "You have any relatives buried here?"

"No," I say, too surprised to lie. "I can't come in if I don't know one of your dead people?"

"Sorry," the grounds guy shrugs. "But you could go up there." He points up the hill toward the highway. I see skinny, old-fashioned tombstones leaning on each other in the weeds. A poor person's auxiliary. Perfect. I've been told that you seldom find anything exciting growing on a rich person's grave. Too much perpetual care.

In among the Hebrew-inscribed gravestones, I find a few English words—Bernstein, Pittsburgh, Kiev—and a few sticky yellow wildflowers. But no roses. I will have to switch faiths.

The next day I go to a Catholic cemetery at the foot of the mountains. This place is so well thought out, right down to plenty of free parking, that it reminds me of a nearby mall. Here, the dead people lie in concentric circles, first a ring of fancy mausoleums, then a ring of important people topped with praying angels, then an endless section of obedient civilians marked by sensible granite blocks. I walk thirty minutes over the lawns before hitting a lode.

Soft salmon-red roses the size of tennis balls cover a granite stone engraved with morning glories and a Russian Orthodox cross. The date of death is 1936 and the inscription reads *Dear Pa.* I whip out my clippers and fall to my knees to search the rose canes for the knobby mark of a graft. There's none that I can see. The plant is woody and thorny, its leaves small with a dull finish—not like the shiny leaves and straight stems of a modern hybrid tea rose. Checking first to see if anyone is watching, I cut several eight-inch sections of Dear Pa and drop them into a Ziploc bag. I will take them home and try to root them into a hedge of roses—a dubious proposition, given my knowledge of these things, but so what. I call it a good day's work.

The next day, I go to Riverside Cemetery, one of Denver's oldest and least maintained, which makes it perfect ground for old roses. Riverside is surrounded by industrial blight—the polluted South Platte, a sloppy joe factory, ragged railyards. Inside its gates are the misfits and eccentrics of Denver history. It is sheltered by huge old trees, crossed by weedy gravel paths and ancient irrigation pipe, dotted with shabby gothic mausoleums. Here and there several picnics are in progress—an old woman in a tailored suit nipping from a Thermos, two heavy metal dudes with sacks from Taco Bell, a private investigator type in dark shades gnawing on a turkey leg. An emaciated runner pounds by, covered in sweat. The graveyard itself has an absentminded air; people are here to do whatever. I know I will find roses.

And I do:

Pauline Bauer Pieper, 1865–1952. A climber, unmistakably old, with white centers and an almost lemony smell.

Mary V. Barger, 1910–1948, and *Grace P. Wist,* 1878–1958. A salmon-pink rose forming such a dense, thorny mat that I can't read the letters on the small stone without pulling apart its canes and cutting up my hands in the process. My first thought is that Mary and Grace were a lesbian couple living in an unenlightened age, but buried side by side. Sure, Grace was thirty-two years older than Mary, but it still could have been love. Or maybe Mary was one of those tuberculosis patients who came to Denver in the first decades of the twentieth century, and Grace was her faithful nurse. Later that night, I phone all the Wists and Bargers in the Denver phone book, just to see if anyone knows the story. But no one has ever heard of either woman.

Baby Logan, 1899—tiny white flowers with a strong rosy perfume. Many, many thorns.

Stonebreaker—a vigorous, woody pink rose with only five petals and a polleny yellow center. No fragrance, but some attitude! It has grown up and through the gravestone, breaking it in half. Only the bottom half—and the words *Gone But Not Forgotten*—remain.

At home, I stick all four of these rose cuttings, as well as Dear Pa, into plastic pots of garden soil. Now all I can do is wait. Frankly, I'll be amazed if these sad little twigs turn into rose bushes, but stranger things have happened, and I have a feeling that if I'm ever going to have a successful relationship with a rose, it will be of the rustled variety. My liaisons with conventional garden roses never work out—I always end up killing them, though I always figure it's no great loss. But that was before I fell in with the Texas Rose Rustlers.

There are plenty of ways to take an interest in old roses. You can zero in on them botanically, or you can fit their stories into the history of your favorite place, or you can simply appreciate the way they act in the land-scape. All these approaches have their proponents—have had, in fact, almost since old roses were new.

But my own attraction to old roses—and the act of rustling—began more in the spirit of plunder. Searching out, digging up, rooting, trad-ing, or otherwise *taking* plants is closely related to thrift-shopping and junking, two sports I play passionately.

I picked Texas for my old rose pilgrimage because Texas is where the art of rustling was invented. The original Texas Rose Rustlers went deep into the province of old ladies, cut a wide swath around the fussiness and classification of the rose world, and found adventure.

At a cafe on the way to the Antique Rose Emporium in Independence, Texas, I fell into a greasy reverie—fried eggs, white toast, home fries, bacon, and all that good bad food—while watching a grizzled short-order cook who had a Marlboro hanging from the corner of her mouth. Two waitresses lounged at opposite ends of the counter. At the tables, people were integrated: half and half, black and white. The pace was slow, verging on tropical.

Back on the road, the heat came at me in a cloud. Crossing the Washington County line took me into a very old part of Texas, the actual headquarters of the Republic during the ten years (1836–1846) when Texas was its own little nation. They were exciting years, and Texans are not about to forget them. Washington County is full of old buildings done up as stores for tourists, selling ducks with ribbons around their necks, historic cheese graters, and constipation remedies left behind by ordinary people of long ago. Restorations are everywhere.

The Antique Rose Emporium (A.R.E.) has four historically correct log cabins on its five-acre grounds, each of them covered with climbing roses, which clamber aggressively into windows, up telephone poles, and over arches. In between the roses are meadows, ponds, winding stone pathways, and perennial beds, all oversized and run-down-on-purpose. It looks as if some very energetic but slightly wild Texan of the Republican period had gone crazy at the local nursery and then died, leaving all his plantings to naturalize however they pleased.

The fact that what you see here you can grow at home is what has made Mike Shoup and his Antique Rose Emporium such a success. The established old rose breeders have been mailing catalogs to the initiated for decades, but if you don't already know roses inside and out, getting through the botanical descriptions and pen-and-ink drawings can be intimidating. So Mike Shoup set up his empire as a place where neophytes could find guidance. Every rose in his vast display gardens has at least a paragraph of simple information attached to it, and each narrow flagstone path leads to a sort of rose diorama. The A.R.E. catalog is full of color photographs and how-to. Best of all, no matter how stunning the rose, Mike won't carry it if it's temperamental.

The approach works. The A.R.E. is currently the country's largest grower of "own-root" roses—ungrafted old garden roses are generally thought to be more authentic. His staff—which once consisted of himself, his wife, and a propagation expert—now number thirty, all of whom stand ready to answer questions, no matter how stupid.

All this leaves Mike little time for rustling roses—unless a TV crew is on hand to record him doing it. Still, he never seems to mind the open-ended discussions of roses into which he's dragged almost daily. To him, talking roses is no more strenuous than gossiping about an eccentric relative. (Like most old rose people, he sees the flowers as almost human. "I have favorites," he told me, "but it wouldn't be fair to the others if I named them.") And then there's always the chance someone will know a rose he hasn't met yet. His best sources, he told me, are older people he encounters on the A.R.E. pathways, lost in memory.

"What it is, is the vehicle of fragrance," Mike said. "Our older customers are really keyed in by it. We find them with tears welling up in their eyes. They tell me, 'I haven't smelled that smell since I was a small child, running in my grandpa's yard.'"

As Mike and I walked through the acres of roses, I tried to find a scent that moved me. No ghosts rose from my memory, but I was struck by the way fragrances curled out onto the paths and drew me in. Nothing smelled sweet and flowery, but there were notes of lemon, apple, and even what I later found out was the smell of fresh tea leaves. At one point a very French, very overpowering smell almost made me dizzy. I can only describe it as *boudoir*.

And there was still more to smell. Mike drove me half a mile east of the Emporium, to the eleven-acre spread that houses his catalog office, greenhouses, and a gently sloped hillside where thousands of potted roses sit in the sun, waiting for wholesalers.

Mike is a big man—a lumberjack/Dad type with a heavy beard—and the heat was killing him. But he walked me through every row of plants on that hill, pinching rose blossoms off plants and tossing them back to me.

"Here's Mermaid," he said, throwing a fragile white rose with a yellow center. "Here's Perle d'Or. Smell it, it's actually kind of rosy smelling, isn't it?"

My hands filled up with flowers. I began stuffing them into my pockets and down the front of my shirt. (When I got undressed that evening, petals fell out.) I could have stayed out on the wholesale hill all day, but Mike was wiping his forehead with a bandanna. He had had enough.

We retreated to his office, an old but refreshingly unrestored house, complete with a sagging porch beneath which a spaniel lay splayed out in the dirt. Inside, old metal desks and the remains of a birthday cake were scattered about. It was about as far as it could be from the deliberately charming atmosphere of the Emporium but a good place to put your feet up and leaf through the selection of old hardback books with the word "rose" in their titles. Before Mike could crack open his Diet Pepsi, though, a visitor arrived.

The man at the door told us his name was Wamon Foster, that he was eighty years old, that he had seen Mike on a TV news show, and that he had driven a hundred miles to get here.

"Can I help you?" Mike asked him.

"Why, no," Wamon Foster replied. "I brung *you* something." He held out a bouquet of roses wrapped in soggy brown paper. "Hit's a deep red old rose," he said. "And I'm fixin' to tell you something. That rose have run all over that washhouse out in back. The fronds done got fourteen foot tall. When I saw you on TV and I said to my wife, why, I'm gon' take that washhouse rose down to him."

Mike tried to figure out what the rose might be. Nine times out of ten, he said, these offerings turn out to be something old, but common. "Does it look like this one?" he asked Mr. Foster, showing him a picture. "No? How about this one here?"

"Hit's way darker than that," Mr. Foster replied, "and it repeats. And you can root it. I took about five, six cuttings last year and stuck 'em in a pot, and then I run off on a trip. And one was living when I come back."

"Do you know anyone else that has one?"

"I do," Mr. Foster said. "Over at the cemetery near us I saw one, and the woman working that grave, that was her grandfather's plot, and he and that rose had been there since 1892."

"Well, we'll root it and see what happens, and let you know," Mike said. "What would you want us to call your rose?"

Mr. Foster seemed a little taken aback. "Why, I'm Wamon Foster," he finally said, "but I surely don't want you to call it the Wamon Foster Rose." Eventually, they settled on Darby Holehausen Cemetery Repeating Red Climber.

After Mr. Foster left, Mike attached a scrawled note to the cuttings and put them in the office refrigerator for his propagator to find. He closed the door on them slowly—they are what matters to him at work. The propagation of roses, he told me, is infinitely more adventuresome than sowing hybrid marigold seeds and watching them turn into bedding plants, which is what he used to do before his life got interesting.

A run-of-the-mill greenhouse made business sense, though, in 1976, the year he left Texas A&M with a horticulture degree. Horticulturists run greenhouses, he thought, and his hometown of Independence seemed as good a place as any to start out.

"It was boom years," he told me. "You couldn't *not* make money in Texas." Mike took the straightforward approach, growing the usual array of marigolds, zinnias, impatiens, and petunias. Five years later he had a blooming business capable of supporting himself, his wife, and three children in style. The next thing he knew, he was "so disenchanted. What I was doing," he said, "was nothing but mass manufacturing."

There seemed to be no way to reconcile his love of hands-in-the-dirt gardening with the business of bedding plants, a business that had been good enough to him that he could hardly afford to cut it off midstream. Finally, he thought he might try raising native Texan plants. If they could survive his county's brutal, windy heat, he thought, they could flourish as landscape plants. Xeriscaping and native gardens were not unheard of in Texas at the time, but they hadn't arrived in his part of the country yet. Wondering whether anyone would pay money for plants some people thought of as weeds made Mike nervous, but he didn't let that stop him.

"I went out into the landscape with my wife, looking for plants we knew would survive," Mike recalled. "We found some perennials, things like dianthus and bouncing bet. But mainly, we saw roses—in cemeteries, old fence rows, abandoned houses. Blooming. Where they *weren't* being cared for."

Until then, Mike had always thought you couldn't grow a rose without fussing over it, which is why he never liked roses much. "I thought they were gaudy and a pain. They got mildew, black spot, aphids . . . but these abandoned roses were different. These roses shouldn't even share the same name."

What Mike came to feel for those tough roses was nothing less than passion. He loved everything about old garden roses—even their less loveable traits.

"They grow like ground cover, like shrubs, like hedges, they even grow up into trees," he told me. Some—the polyanthas and chinas, in particular—bloom all season. Others flower for only a few weeks in spring, and then, just to be difficult, break out in hooked thorns. Old rose fragrances are persistent, and their ability to survive disease and neglect is remarkable. And yet, as far as Mike could tell, most of the roses he found were headed for extinction.

"What happened was that breeders in the forties and fifties stopped caring about anything but the flowers," Mike said. "They wanted the flowers perfect, for winning shows and all that. Along the way, they bred out disease resistance, fragrance, and beauty of form. People who grew roses began to put them in straight lines so they could be sprayed every day. But you go back to the old periodicals, and you find pictures of roses completely covering a house, wild in the landscape."

Perhaps it was that tendency that breeders hoped to tone down. In 1867, when hybrid teas were first developed, they indeed seemed to be a breakthrough, blooming repeatedly all season, with strong rather than floppy necks and just one bloom per stem. The roses themselves had a new look—they unfolded slowly, from a tight ball of bud, like tulips, instead of exploding open, shedding petals along the way, as they had in the past.

The result was the perfect flower to stick in a vase—but not the kind of flower that got Mike excited. What he wanted was "a return to wildness, in the landscape, and in the roses."

In the ensuing two years, Mike collected about a hundred "found" roses, which he placed in the hands of a university-trained propagator. Not that old roses always needed such coddling. Many of the gardeners Mike collected roses from could propagate almost in their sleep.

"One of my first rustles was a Louis-Philippe red china rose I got from old Mrs. Meyer," he said. "She had gotten that rose from her mother, and her two sisters were the only other people in town who had it."

Old Mrs. Meyer had no idea that the Louis-Philippe rose was brought to Texas from France in 1834 by Lorenzo de Zavala, the Mexican ambassador. She didn't care, either. She just stuck cuttings in the ground and grew the thing.

"None of these people had a horticultural education, and it didn't matter. Year after year," Mike marveled, "they applied their common sense."

When no one could offer registered names for the old roses he found, Mike invented his own. He christened Red Burglar—a thorny climber that had actually trapped a thief trying to enter an old woman's house—and Highway 290 Pink Buttons, rustled by the road's shoulder. There was the Martha Gonzales rose, which had grown in Mike's hometown ever since old Mrs. Gonzales could remember, in soil so terrible it hadn't produced a blade of grass in decades. All three, plus some ninety more rustled roses, were listed in Mike's first catalog, issued in 1984.

Technically, the roses he offers are not antique—a term that applies only to roses bred before 1867, the year hybrid teas were developed—

nor even necessarily old. They merely have to have old garden rose qualities. The point is not to produce perfect roses at perfect intervals, but to fill the landscape with something beautifully carefree—in the form of roses even a scatterbrained gardener could grow.

Mike remembers the first catalog as expensive to produce and "pretty rinky-dink" in quality, but customers responded to its complete growing instructions and close-up color photographs of every rose listed. You didn't have to be an expert to understand it, and Mike offered his readers something entirely new—a service to which gardeners could send clippings, which were then propagated and grown until they bloomed, at which point the A.R.E. staff either identified them as historical roses or gave them new names. (Some of these donated roses are mainstays of the catalog today.) News of the rose detective agency spread through Texas, where it soon came to the attention of two women who'd been rustling roses when Mike was still in college.

"They'd been at it before anyone else," he says of Pam Puryear and Margaret Sharpe. "They were the original players." Players is right. Pam Puryear and Margaret Sharpe were the first to play this scientific pursuit as a game.

❧ ☀ ❧

At the end of June, I reach Pam Puryear by phone. It is, she tells me, the beginning of air-conditioning and the end of rose rustling until fall.

"It's just too hot," she says breathlessly, in a deep Southern drawl. "The hollyhocks are ten feet tall, you cain't hardly see the blooms, and I am just *fighting* with the weeds. I've got herbs growing in our old clay tennis court, it's from 1912, you know, with eight inches of cinders and the drainage is just perfect. Boy howdy, you cain't fertilize it, though, it goes right through to the Gulf of Mexico that same day."

Miz Puryear could happily spend hours going off on any number of tangents—from old tennis court design to erosional trends in Texas. Over the years, she has written scholarly monographs for university presses on such disparate topics as Victorian women's underwear and the history of steamboating on the Brazos River. She is the type of person, who, when discussing the fifties, usually means the 1850s.

Pam casts herself as the unmarried high school English teacher in her late forties, faint of health, vaguely eccentric, and still living among the ruins of the Puryear estate, built by her great-grandfather in 1869.

"It sounds wonderful, I know, but it's all falling down," she says. "I live alone with my widowed mother and twenty-three fat cats." Having given up teaching ten years ago—"high blood pressure troubles," she says—she now works behind the counter "scaring tourists" at an antique store. The job barely pays the bills, but Pam isn't worried. "I picked out a rich man to marry and I got to finally go over to his place and tell him about it," she explains.

If that plan falls through, though, she's content to become a character in her own family history, known for her ceaseless pottering in the circa 1871 greenhouse. Like the rest of her family compound, it's headed back into the dirt, but Pam can think of worse fates. You can grow things in dirt, and doing that is in her blood.

"It's an obsession, all right," she agrees, "if an obsession is an inordinate desire. My grandmother taught me about gardening. She taught me that if you skim the weeds off the top, they'll come back up from the bottom. She was very Victorian. Her ideal was vast expanses of lawn with specimen shrubs dotted around—red, pink, red, pink. She didn't have *bad* taste, she had *no* taste."

Under her grandmother's direction, Pam dabbled in annual flowers and herbs—even a few roses, but they made her frantic. "Hybrid teas are impossible," she recalls. "They're made for cool, wet summers, and around here we generally have three cold days and a heck of a lot of hot ones. Hybrid teas take one look at that and commit suicide."

Throughout her teens and early twenties, Pam struggled with them anyway, "taking their little pHs, fussing with their soil," until one day in 1970, when she took a trip through the countryside looking for old buildings.

"We went to see a wonderful 1822 log house up on a bluff," she remembers. "It was about to be moved off the site and lord, it was covered with clapboard and no one had lived there since 1940. Out front were two old rose bushes. Here it was August, in the middle of a three-year drought, and these rose bushes were blooming their heads off. I thought, what am I doing trying to pamper my roses when this one here ain't even been cared for since 1940?"

A few days later, Pam went back and dug the plants up. She gave one to the woman who owned the land, planted one in her own backyard, and gave some cuttings to a friend. "And those cuttings became a hundred-and-twenty-foot hedge that stopped traffic," she says. "That old rose rooted like a sweet potato."

Which is probably why she began to notice it all over the county. People told her it was called Old Pink Daily or Common Monthly. Her own horticultural research revealed its real name: Old Blush. It had first come to Europe from China in 1752, and, as far as she could tell, it had come to Texas from Europe, its cuttings kept moist in a wet towel or a raw potato.

Old Blush made Pam crazy for old roses—"because it pleases the viewer," she says, "and you don't have to give up your life to please *it*." Certain that there were other sympathetic roses to be had, Pam read all the old rose journals and catalogs she could find, and when she got tired of reading, she designed and built "an extremely primitive misting system to help root cuttings." But that slow, deliberate act struck Pam as something of a letdown compared with the thrill of hunting roses. "I tell you," she says, "it was a relief when Mike started up and I could just bring my little cuttings to him and let him do the propagating."

She joined the Heritage Rose Society, the biggest American organization for old rose fanciers, as well as the more hybrid-tea-focused American Rose Society. It was at one of the A.R.S. meetings in Houston that she met Margaret Sharpe.

"Old roses are a tight world," Pam says. "Pretty soon, you know everyone. You may mention my name in Australia, and a rose person will know who I am."

Margaret Sharpe, however, was not just any rose person. "Some people are in it to make collections, but not me," she states. "Some people are looking for a particular type of a particular rose. My way is when I see a pretty rose that would look pretty in my yard, I start me a cup and grow it till I get tired of it."

Margaret has grown roses ever since 1944, the year she married and moved into her first home in Corpus Christi. Having four children did not stop her from the serious cultivation of hybrid teas. "I kept my kids out there in the yard with me," she recalls. "They learned enough gardening that by the time they were teenagers, they all did it for the neighbors, for money." The approach she taught them was anything but finicky.

"I believe in just taking my cup of coffee and my clippers out to the garden in the morning and snip here and snip there," she says. "Do what you want. That way, there's never this awful feeling that the fourteenth of February is Valentine's Day and your roses must be fed promptly on Valentine's Day. People's lives are regimented enough without all that."

She did well with her Zen approach. By the time the Sharpes moved to Houston in 1977, Margaret had won "about every award there is" and been appointed a life consulting rosarian by the American Rose Society. This title "means they think I'm doing all right," Margaret says, and it allows her to judge any A.R.S. show in the country, any time she feels like it. But by the time of the move to Houston, she says, she didn't much feel like it.

"I quickly found out that Houston has the largest rose society in the world," she recalls. "They had quite a few consulting rosarians already." The idea of being one of the crowd did not appeal to Margaret. "I said, 'Where do I fit into all this?'" The society decided she could be trusted to find a few antique roses to grace Houston's historic government buildings.

Obligingly, Margaret struck out into that new territory. With the sesquicentennial anniversary of the Republic of Texas coming up, she decided she'd try to find out which roses were popular during the Republican period and which, if any, were still blooming 150 years later. Once out on the road, she immediately began to take cuttings.

"You have to—it's only normal," she says. "It's no different than taking the smell from a rose. Then you take a paper cup and some clean soil and stick it! There's no trick to it. Just keep aware."

Like Pam Puryear and Mike Shoup, Margaret Sharpe was captivated by the ability of old roses to thrive through adversity and neglect. Because she and Pam were seeking essentially the same thing, they became rose-hunting companions.

"We were all over the countryside," Pam remembers of those early days. "We haunted the old cemeteries, where the roses had been surviving for eons, and we gave ourselves a nice, highfalutin' name."

Even though they were now the Brazos Symposium on Old Roses, their mission was firmly rooted in the earth. They couldn't have tracked down their roses, for instance, without blending into the tapestry of gossip they found in every small town. They both came around so often, displaying so much patience and fascination, that people usually told them whatever they wanted to know.

"I particularly remember a tiny German bakery over by Highway Ten," Margaret says. "There was just one old rose in the whole town, and it was the prettiest purple—a gorgeous thing that had really struggled. We went back there two, three times trying to discover what it was. And finally"—on the strength of repeat visits—"we learned that the old bakery was one house out of several that had once belonged to four sisters, who had homes on the remains of their family land. Long about 1910, all four had hundreds of those purple roses. This was the only one that survived."

No one ever figured out the real name of that purple rose—but the little they knew was enough for Margaret Sharpe, who grew a cutting in her yard and called it Corner Bakery Rose.

"It was the two of us and anyone else we could drag up," Margaret recalls. "We'd find roses growing away down in the middle of nowhere, cows eating them down, and they just kept growing. We were very taken with that."

"We'd go to these little old towns and cruise the streets in September or October, looking for roses that were still flush," Pam remembers. "Then we'd go back in November when it was cool, with an ice chest. You cain't root a rose too well until the weather cools off."

Into the waiting Mason jars went cuttings of roses that later turned out to be two-thousand-year old Gallica strains. In went the Little Food Market Rose, later identified by Pam as a very refined polyantha rose from 1890 called Clotilde Soupert. In went the Hole Rose—"We found it growing in a hole," Margaret explains—along with Emma West and Emma East, cut from the east and west sides of a house belonging to a woman named Emma.

Like Mike, they had their best luck in towns and cemeteries on the wrong side of the tracks. "Rich people's graves have the hybrid teas from the garden center," Margaret explains. "Poor and ethnic people, they don't give a damn what the American Rose Society recommends. In the Mexican sections, Old Blush is all over, all wound up among the graves. You have to hope the care isn't very good. Otherwise, the city hires these butchers who hack the roses down."

On babies' tiny graves, they found old roses cultivated for their tiny flowers. They found the Memorial Rose, a white "running" rose—a climber, in other words, with nothing to climb up. (Along the way, both decided the time they were spending as live inhabitants of cemeteries was enough. Neither wishes to be buried in a graveyard, with or without a rose. "I'd rather be cremated and end up as fertilizer," Margaret says.)

By the second year of hunting, both women had a surplus of rooted plants, which they began trading with a like-minded "bunch from Dallas."

"Everyone would meet up at my house and we'd all bring Ziploc bags full of cuttings and rooted plants and we'd swap," Pam says. "After that, we'd start rustling in a caravan."

They were welcome almost everywhere they went.

"We'd get permission, of course," Margaret says. "Once, we were walking through a field and a neighbor farmer caught sight of us. He wanted to know what we thought we were doing. 'Looking for roses,' I said. He says, 'A likely story and I suggest you just get right off this property,' and he brandished a shotgun! Well, we didn't argue with that, but afterwards we laughed and laughed."

Margaret's friends, who heard the story over and over again, wanted to know if she really intended to subject herself to such dangers. "Well," she remembers saying, in her finest gunfighter drawl, "I still like roses. I think I might just go rustle up a few."

That's how the Brazos Symposium turned into the Texas Rose Rustlers, whose logo features an armadillo-riding cowboy wielding clippers. The whole concept was a breath of fresh air in rarified rose circles, and rose rustling took off. Today, there are 225 registered rose rustlers in Texas, all of whom pay seven dollars per year for the *Old Texas Rose* newsletter and directions to the latest rose-gathering ground. "But thousands more show up to the rustles," Margaret adds. "We're not very official. We just take people in—we don't even care if we have your money or not." Soon, the idea of a quiet rustle among friends was all but extinct.

"By 1984, we'd have eighty cars at a time show up for rustles," Pam says. "Once we lost half of 'em at a stoplight and never did find them."

"It's been an adventure," Margaret agrees, "quite a shocking adventure. Out in the country, people see all these cars coming and they think it's a funeral. The little children run around, whispering, 'Who died?' and wondering who we are. Well, we're all different kinds, some black, some white, some Hispanic, some in their teens, and some in their eighties and nineties, and we all get out and go around together. We're immediately friends," she says, "we immediately have common ground."

❦ ☼ ❦

A few months after my trip to the Antique Rose Emporium, I passed through Anderson, Texas, on my way to western Louisiana. Pam Puryear was there, scaring tourists as promised, and a few locals as well. On the way to lunch, she led me right under the nose of a moving school bus, which set up a terrible honking, and caused her to search for a hankie.

"This is, of course, the noon rush," she said, guiding me through the nearly deserted, and very old, streets of Anderson. We came to a roadside cafe, where we ate chicken-fried steak—"If it's bad for you, give it here," Pam said—and talked about gardening at a breathless clip. Pam told me her favorite gardening outfit consists of "this old blue calico dress, real long so I can bend over with impunity, but it done got so thin you can read a newspaper through it." Her favorite tool is a little aluminum hook, almost like a dentist's scraper, which she calls "the Nitpicker." "I would not allow a loan of it to my best friend for ten seconds," she stated categorically.

After lunch, we went to a graveyard where Old Blush has been known to bloom, but it was too late in the year. No matter. Pam was able to indulge a brand new obsession—the rescue of plastic flowers from cemetery dumpsters. "I'm a ghoul," she said cheerfully, "which, if you think about it, ranks pretty low in the social structure. What I do with these flowers is, I make awful hats, covered with dripping greenery, to wear to garden club meetings. If you give me five dollars for the hat and the tulle, I'll make you one. It'll be horrible," she promised.

𝕮 ☀ 𝕭

While I wait for the hat to arrive by UPS; and for the Texas Rose Rustlers' annual Pearl Harbor Day rustle; and for the next fascinating cemetery to come along; and for Dear Pa to either root or die, I've been thinking about old roses, wondering what it is about them that keeps me—and so many others—interested. There's no denying that they are somehow a cut above other flowers. I have practically no memory, for instance, of the smell of the florist roses that sat on my desk all last week. And yet twenty-eight years ago, when I was seven, I ran across a white rose bush in an abandoned lot, growing through the remains of an old boat house, and its fragrance still tantalizes me. What was that unroselike smell—maple syrup?

Identifying that smell—and that rose—strikes me as an eminently worthwhile pursuit. I think this is because being around old roses is good for me. Old roses, by example, are full of instructions on how to live right. They stand for certain things I like to consider true. Such as:

1. There is more than one way to be beautiful.

2. Survival is a noble goal.

3. Good climates are in the eye of the beholder, not the tourism board.

4. If you are attacked by disease, abandonment, or a bad chain of events, do not necessarily despair. There is always the chance you were bred to be tough.

5. Everyone should not smell the same.

2 Heat

"Try a chili with it, Miss Sharp," said
Joseph, really interested.

"A chili," said Rebecca, gasping.
"Oh yes!" She thought a chili was something cool, as its name imported, and was
served with some. "How fresh and green
they look," she said, and put one in her
mouth. It was hotter than the curry; flesh
and blood could bear it no longer. She laid
down her fork. "Water, for Heaven's
sake, water!" she cried.

WILLIAM MAKEPEACE THACKERAY, VANITY FAIR

On the edge of Vigil's service station, where the basketcase cars rot slowly into the ground, Willy Martinez is selling roasted chile. As I ride by on my motorcycle, I pass through a cloud of the most mouthwatering smells on earth. It is welded in my mind to a high, blue sky, twiggy marigolds bitten by frost, and the Back-to-School sale at Kmart. The smell of roasted New Mexico chile is *why* it is autumn in North Denver.

"Twenty years ago, nobody knew the New Mexico chile," Willy Martinez says. "It actually started with me."

Willy is a big man, in his fifties, dressed in old jeans and a button-down shirt with the buttons bulging around his stomach. Leaning against a dirty white van parked behind a makeshift tent, he watches his four part-time employees as they sell and roast chile, talking manically to the customers and each other.

Driving north on Federal Boulevard, I have noticed at least twenty other stands just like this one, each trying to outdo the other with hand-lettered signs on neon posterboard. Yet all this began with Willy Martinez, who would rather soak up sun and talk sparingly than engage in a hard sell.

"Yeah, I'm the source," he says. "I been messing around with chile forever. It was a friend of mine from down in Hatch, New Mexico, told me it was a big market. The first year I sold it from a walk-in cooler behind my house on Wyandot. I don't know how they found out about it, but a lot of people came to the cooler and bought chile. I've been messing with Sandia and the Six-Four chile, and people, they are just buying and buying."

At this stand, anyway, they are. Maybe it is because Charles Gurule, Willy's business partner, is letting them taste first.

"Go ahead," he tells a slow-moving man in a straw cowboy hat and pointy boots. "Taste the vein, man, it's the hottest part."

Slow Man tastes, sweats a little, wipes his forehead, and commits to three bushels of NuMex Big Jim peppers. Charles dumps them into the roaster—a perforated forty-gallon oil drum on its side that turns the chile like a chicken on a spit. Squatting on his heels, Slow Man waits. Charles passes the time by cracking piñon nuts with his front teeth and disparaging an unscrupulous chile farmer he met on his last buying trip to New Mexico.

"Whatever works for him, I guess," he tells a coworker. "He's the kind of guy who will look at you straight and tell you his chile is hot as hell, and it isn't. One time he shows me a *Polaroid* of a chile. I don't want to see no *Polaroid*."

"You want the real thing," says the coworker.

"Give me the real thing," Charles agrees. "If you lie to people about chile they'll cuss you out for a year and remember you next fall."

I believe it. A seemingly huge percentage of Northwest Denver people survive winter on the strength of the plastic bags full of roasted chile they keep in their freezers.

"You just go ahead and take ten or twelve chiles out of the bag and put them under the faucet," Willy Martinez explains. "You let it thaw out and peel it and put it on your hamburger, or cook it without nothing, it depends on how you like it. Just don't try to peel it all at once, it'll burn your hands."

But there are as many methods of handling peppers as there are people who eat them. Some of my neighbors, armed with disposable gloves, *do* peel the whole bushel before chopping it up into different kinds of salsa. An admitted lightweight, I still can thirty or forty pints of salsa each fall—and run out by February. And I always keep a few bags of whole roasted chiles in the freezer. When the diminishing light of winter begins to get to me, I put some chopped chile in my scrambled eggs or chicken soup, breathing its inimitable *calor* through a runny nose. I don't question the assumption that chiles cure everything from hangovers to asthma. I don't question chiles at all. They grow where lettuce fears to tread, wilting and unloved in crummy soil, but ultimately successful. I can't conceive of living in the West and *not* growing chile.

This is because of the Perez family.

Farms breed stuff—and, in deciding what to do with it all, farmers tend to fall into one of two camps. Either they let it all wash up like a tide against their fences—waves of rusting machinery, stray weed patches, abandoned chicken houses—or they can fight every inch of decay, which is how Alex Perez did it, and how his children continue to do it.

I found out about the Perez family from eating at their restaurant, the Bamboo Hut, located on the north end of downtown Denver's skid row. There was never anything remotely Polynesian about the Bamboo Hut but its name. It is a standard, no-frills Mexican place, except for its green chili, a hot, thin juice that clears sinuses faster than any prescription. What makes it special, I heard, was the raw material—chile grown by the Perezes on their family land in Commerce City.

Commerce City is the kind of close-in suburb that radio talk-show hosts love to hate. It has more than its share of industrial blight and smell, not to mention several square miles of unsightly gasworks. But it also has the kind of modest acreage small-time truck farmers can afford. Alex Perez, Sr., bought this land in 1949, and his wife, Marcelline, still lives here, along with her forty-one-year-old son, Albert, who moved back home after his divorce. Two years ago, they let me hang around at the beginning of the chile season.

It was early May. The pepper plants, Anaheims and jalapeños, were waiting out the frost date in cold frames made from recycled windows. Albert was worried about them.

"They don't have the stamina, I don't think," he said. "I don't know if it's because of the heat or because of that thing where they tell you to put lotion on—that greenhouse effect. It seems like nothing wants to grow."

He was trying to figure out the best way to get nitrogen to the six-inch-tall plants, in hopes of getting them to leaf out faster. They looked perfectly healthy to me, but then, it was unseasonably hot, and peppers like that.

Albert went out to work on an old tractor, perfectly maintained according to his father's rules, even though his father had died six months before, and the farm had ceased to be a commercial enterprise.

"But we keep it going to honor my Dad," Albert's brother Alex Perez, Jr. (known as J. R.), had told me. "We could buy chile cheaper than it costs us to grow, but we do it for him."

Alex Perez's formidable presence was everywhere.

"This is his locker from when he worked on the railroad," Albert told me, as we walked around the five acres. The locker looked more like an old wooden steamer trunk. Devoid of clothes or tools, it stood outside under the sun, alone. "Full of his memories, he said, so they gave it to him when he retired. And those are his shoes."

I looked above the door of a small building once used to house Mexican nationals who came to harvest chile, and indeed saw two well-worn, sturdy shoes nailed to the wall. Above them, Alex, Sr., had written: *Que hombre podra llenar estos zapatos?*

What man could fill these shoes?

"No one," Albert said emphatically, "that's for sure."

Then he told me the legend of his father—how he was born in Texas, raised by a stingy maiden aunt, and supported himself by the time he was twelve. His wife, Marcelline, one of nine children whose mother died early of influenza, already had two children when she married Alex Perez. Together, they moved to Denver in the forties, produced eight children in rapid succession, and ran a hotel in the predominately black Five Points area.

"When there was a shooting," J. R. remembered, "we'd shut the lights off and wait till the police came. My oldest brother was only eighteen when he was shot dead in some kind of gang thing. My dad decided he had to get us out of the city."

With proceeds from his job as a railroad mechanic, Alex Perez bought the Commerce City land, with an eye toward growing chile. Not during working hours, of course, but in the intervening time between coming home and going to sleep. He expected—demanded—that his wife and children work the same schedule.

"The house here, it was nothing but a basement, and all of us lived down there until we could help my dad build the house on top," J. R. recalled.

"My husband tell me I have to move out here and I cry and cry," eighty-year-old Marcelline related. "We didn't have heat, no water or nothing, a well forty-five feet from the house. And it wasn't much of a house."

"And the land," Albert added, "it was nothing but a horse pasture."

Born in 1950, Albert was the first child to be raised entirely on the farm, working with his brothers and sisters whenever he wasn't in school or asleep. "Dad wasn't an easy guy to get along with," he said bluntly. "He made the girls jump in and feed the hogs before school. He didn't like us running around. He never let me go to my prom or my graduation parties. He didn't approve of that stuff, and besides, I had to be up early in the morning and ready to go."

"A memory I can't get rid of," J. R. added, "is of one of my uncles coming by on a Sunday with a picnic basket and he wanted to take us kids with him, and my dad said, no, and we had to stay home weeding the chile. 'I don't like for the work to pile up around here,' my Dad said."

Although Alex Perez never posted a sign in front of his farm, every fall customers would appear and the children would be sent to the fields to pick peppers one bushel at a time. Her daughters helped Marcelline can hundreds of quarts of chile—pickled and roasted and made into salsa. The closest Alex ever came to advertising was to command Marcelline to place a quart of pickled peppers on the kitchen table, where accounts were settled.

"They saw those cans, they bought them," Marcelline confirms. She saw very little of the proceeds. Alex did not believe in squandering money on such things as entertainment, drinking, or unnecessary kitchen appliances. (Marcelline just got her first microwave, which she loves.)

"What we almost all did was get married and take off to the city," Albert recalled. "That's what you had to do."

This did not relieve their obligation to return to the farm during the planting and harvesting of chile. All eight Perezes considered that something of a sacred duty, and several eventually went into the restaurant business, which meant they were expected to buy chile—at whatever price—from their father.

By 1991 the Perez children, who had their own teenagers to contend with, were beginning to rethink their resentment. Alex had done what he could to keep them off the streets, and it had worked. More lenient parenting, J. R. told me once, had proved disappointing. He sometimes wondered, he said, if his children understood the work ethic at all.

As if to underscore this point, Alex, Sr., was literally too busy to die on Christmas Day, 1991, when he was felled by a heart attack. He still had some farm implements to tidy up for winter, and he got out of bed and did it, despite his pain. That accomplished, he died two days later.

The pressure eased—somewhat.

"My Dad didn't approve of parties and drinking," J. R. said, "but now that he's gone, I give a big one in October, right when we harvest the last of the chile. I hire a Mexican band and we roast a pig and have a few beers." The party rollicks on in a building Alex built for butchering hogs, and everyone has a good time—none more so than Marcelline, who discovered a thirst for the outside world when Alex died.

"I go everywhere," she said. "To my son's bar for Sunday breakfast, and I sit right up front. To church when I feel like it. To the mall, whenever someone says they'll drive me. I love to go."

"I like it, living with her," Albert said, while also admitting that he and his mother don't always agree on what TV shows to watch. "But I don't have time for it anyway," he added, "not when I got all this work to do."

The May Saturday traditionally reserved for Perez family chile planting was only five days away. "They *all* come," Albert said, "forty or so, and they all complain their backs hurt when the day is over. They're not used to it anymore."

A hint of disgust crept into Albert's voice. Is this what his father sounded like?

"Oh maybe," Albert laughed, "I just know with peppers, you have to be the type. For me, it's working at my own pace, it relieves my tension and loneliness. It works on my mind."

And then he went back to work on his chile. He went out for a load of chicken manure—"Hoo, talk about some ripe stuff," he said, with glee. He planted a row of carrots next to where Anaheims would be set—in the hope of getting *muy picante* carrots. He talked with his brother about withholding water from the plants so that they would wilt. "They get hotter that way. And the ones you pick right before the frost, those are the hottest," he told me.

Just then, a man in a fancy car pulled up. He had come from twenty miles away, in spite of the lack of any sign advertising Plants for Sale, to purchase ten seedlings.

"You got garden centers near you," Albert pointed out. "Why do you come here?"

"I just do," the man said, reaching for his wallet.

I went home with a quart of Marcelline's pickled peppers and set out twelve seedlings of my own. Since then, I have grown whatever hot pepper catches my eye—from killer habañeros to almost biteless Anaheim milds—and mix them together indiscriminately. I suppose I am a chile generalist, but now that I know the Perezes, I know that a serious interest in chile is simply beyond my abilities, let alone my soft moral fiber. So I grow them, and eat them, and enjoy the heat of the moment.

Everything I know about peppers is wrong.

"Hot carrots," says Dr. Heather Graham. "Well, I don't think so. I don't know about that wilting theory, either. I don't know that wilting would affect the taste or the pungency."

As for the Perez rule that the peppers picked right before frost are the hottest—Dr. Heather says it works in exactly the opposite way, just as green peppers are almost always hotter before they turn red. I have to take Dr. Heather's word for this because she is Vegetable Specialist at New Mexico State University in Las Cruces, and the chile lab where she works is acknowledged to be the world's most expert. It was here that several essential chile peppers (the Anaheim, the NuMex R. Naky, the NuMex Big Jim) were developed. This is where western chile growers turn when they need a hand. The research being done here is at least partly responsible for the incredible surge in popularity the chile pepper has experienced in the past twenty years. Acreage used to grow it commercially nearly tripled between 1975 and 1989, and new varieties were introduced yearly.

A transplant from South Carolina, Dr. Heather was amazed at the zeal with which New Mexico scientists pursue knowledge of chile.

"This is my first year on the job," she says. "I had my Master's and Ph.D. in horticulture and plant physiology. I had worked with tomatoes and green beans. But nothing has been like this. The first couple weeks, the people here took me out for so much Mexican food I had major stomach problems. I had to eat cheese sandwiches and yogurt after *that* initiation. But then," she says, "I started to crave it. They've been growing chile in this valley for a long, long time. It's kind of *in* the culture here."

A few days after talking to Dr. Heather on the phone, I receive a weighty package in the mail—a complete trousseau of specialized chile publications. In spite of the technical language, I learn that the heat of chile comes from an alkaloid called capsaicin, which resides mainly in the placenta tissue, the white "ribs" that hold the seeds inside each pepper. Degree of heat is measured in something known as Scoville units. A completely heatless pepper—a paprika, say, or a Yolo Wonder Bell pepper—would be a zero on this scale, while habañeros, the world's hottest peppers, rate between two hundred and three hundred thousand units.

"A lot has to do with climate, too," Dr. Heather says, when I call her back. "Environmental stress affects heat and pungency. Too many hot days and cool nights, and not enough water."

"But that sounds just like New Mexico," I say.

"Oh yeah," Dr. Heather agrees, "and all that makes peppers hotter on the Scoville scale."

Part of her job is to determine how hot peppers are—by tasting them but also with the aid of something called High Pressure Liquid Chromatography, which helps scientists gauge the amount of capsaicin in a given pepper. The varieties appear to be endless—both because of the chile's tendency to cross-pollinate at the drop of a hat, and because many New Mexican farmers prefer *nativos* to commercial seed.

"All that means is they're saving seed from a particular region and a particular cross-pollination," Dr. Heather explains. This is how individual farmers can produce such hard-to-duplicate tastes. Beyond that, says Dr. Heather, chile lovers develop partisan preferences between peppers from north of Santa Fe and those from Hatch Valley, whose southern tip is just twenty-five miles from old Mexico and the Texas border towns. "I don't know which is more popular," she says, "but the Hatch Valley is sometimes referred to as the chile capital of the world."

But before I settle on a visit to Hatch, I decide I need to talk to someone who has traveled the length and breadth of New Mexico. I call Sam'l P. Arnold, a chef/ad man/entrepreneur who runs a restaurant in the foothills west of Denver known as The Fort. The Fort is always turning up in national cooking magazines—as well as *People* and the *New York Times*—because nowhere else will you find a cuisine quite as Western.

It began when he moved from Pittsburgh to Santa Fe in 1948, "because," he says, "no one would hire me to do anything. You're always either too young or too old. So I came west and started a toy store next to a Mexican restaurant owned by my landlord, Luis Salazar."

Mr. Salazar's restaurant was where Sam first became fascinated with authentic frontier cooking—posole, blue corn, and chile—and he still gets rhapsodic when he remembers a recipe from those days. "The blue corn tortilla enchiladas, always flat, never rolled, with a sprinkling of cheese and onions, and *flooded* with good, good red chile. And maybe pop a fried egg on the top of it," he recalls. "I soon learned that Santa Fe had just two months of business, July and August, and the other ten months, we starved. I learned to eat enchiladas at Mr. Salazar's for forty-five cents."

In 1950, after meticulous research into the old West, the Santa Fe Trail, and Native American customs, Sam moved to Denver, started an ad agency, and built The Fort as a replica of William Bent's 1840s-era adobe trading post. Passing through its courtyard on my way in to a dinner table, I have seen such things as a live bear, an open fire in front of a tepee, and a troupe of drunken mountain men who mostly turned out to be waiters. Once inside, I have eaten pork chops with red chiles, jalapeños stuffed with peanut butter and more chile, and even chile in my drinking whiskey. Sam'l P. Arnold *loves* chile. He is the reigning *queso grande* (big cheese) of an obscure organization known as the International Connoisseurs of Green and Red Chile. (Their favorite toast, spoken while rattling a dried chile pepper overhead, is "Up your pod!") Sam has yet to make a Chile Swirl ice-cream flavor, but it is probably only a matter of time. Naturally, he has been all over New Mexico in search of the perfect pod.

"Well, Hatch chile," he says politely. "It's nice. But with New Mexico chile, there's a big difference between Rio Arriba [the north], and Rio Abajo [the South]. If you stay northwest, around Chimayo and Dixon, they have some seed there that I think is the Rolls Royce of the taste. It is a bolder, sharper flavor, yet more lingering. Well," he concludes, "it is absolutely soul-delighting."

Sam tasted twenty-three different powdered New Mexico chiles to find his favorite—a very local variety known as Dixon Medium Mild, and though he imports it by the sixty-pound sack, he never gets tired of the smell of it. "No," he says, "when you cook your roux until it's actually something like a little pancake, and you add your chile, and then break it with chicken broth and a great blast of chile steam comes out, oh boy, you don't want to have your nose over the pot unless you want to have it well-cleared."

But Sam's nose is always over a pot of chile, even when he's out of the country. On their way to England's Scilly Isles last fall, he and his wife brought along bottles of chile sauce and small tubs of red chile powder. "You get so addicted," he says. "There is no meal without chile."

A year goes by measured in chile—forty-five quarts of salsa and half a Hefty trash bag full of roasted Anaheims—and when fall comes again, I stop by Vigil's to see if Willy Martinez is in action again. Not this time. His former associates say he has stopped messing with chile for the time being and is deep into a scheme to import Peñafiel and other ultra-sweet Mexican soft drinks.

But Charles Gurule and his two-year-old son, E. J., are running the stand. E. J. is busy climbing the fifty-pound burlap sacks of piñons that are stacked up on the pavement. It is up to the five or six itinerant chile salesmen Charles has hired for the season to keep an eye on him—to make sure he doesn't get his hands covered with chile oil, run under someone's pickup, or choke on a piñon. As child care challenges go, though, this one isn't bad: E. J. is a mild-mannered child, suited to the lifestyle of his father, the chile baron. He responds amenably to Spanish or English.

Once a week almost since birth, E. J.'s made the trip from Denver down to the Mexico/New Mexico border, overnight, by car. He sits patiently through miles of Mexican railroad, amusing himself while his father rides herd on a boxcar load of chile bound for Denver.

"You just have to know how to handle kids," Charles says, enjoying the role of expert—on children, or chile, whatever. Right now, while preparing E. J.'s bottle, he talks chile to anyone who will listen.

"Mild," he snorts. "There is no mild. Mild is hot." Everything else, he says, is hotter. He should know. After the fall season dies down, he'll go back to his regular job as owner and proprietor of the Big Chili, a small storefront specializing in more than one hundred different varieties of dried and ground chile from all over the world. Since I last saw Charles, the Big Chili has burgeoned as a mail-order business that sells hot ground peppers and salsas to customers in forty states. But Charles hasn't even unlocked its doors in weeks. He's been too busy making the 800-mile round trip to Hatch, bringing back flatbed loads of peppers in sacks.

Charles's favorite chile farmer—one of the few, he says, who will tell the truth about his chile—is Angel Baquerra of Arrey, a small town at the south end of the forty-mile-long Hatch Valley.

"He worked in the chile fields, with his father and his brothers; he's been doing it all his life," Charles says of Angel. "But he has some radical ideas—like fertilizing, crop rotation, and not picking too many times in a season. His two sisters run a grocery store and a restaurant in their little town. Hell," he says, "Angel's known all the way to Walsenburg."

At the end of October, as the last of the red chile sells out in Denver, I start to drive south. I hope to follow the line of yellow where the aspens are turning, to meet fall on its way north, ride with it for a few miles, then continue south until I pass the pepper harvest and end up back in summer. On the way to New Mexico I take small roads with snowy mountains shimmering on their edges. I sleep in campgrounds, one so beautiful and lonely that I could stay a week if it weren't for the smell of the mothballs I have to sprinkle around my tent and car to keep away the bears, who have spent the autumn ripping apart utility sheds, apple trees, and house pets.

Three hours after leaving bear country, I cross the Colorado/New Mexico border. Suddenly I am in a land of red earth, blue sky, yellow trees. The towns I pass through are poor, but astonishingly beautiful, with adobe houses trimmed in intense Caribbean colors, and rows of red chile drying on roofs. At a gas station, the green-eyed boy who takes my money speaks only Spanish. At a restaurant, the Hispanic-looking waiters speak English with a singsong accent, but know only the important Mexican words: curses, food, and song lyrics.

By eight the next morning, I am sitting in the front seat of Angel Baquerra's beat-up black pickup truck. Between us is a .22 rifle with which he hopes to shoot a few rabbits for his dogs' dinner, if there's time.

"We're in the middle of harvesting chile," he explains. "We don't have any days off. I haven't been fishing, I don't think, since I was fifteen years old."

This is true, too, of the rest of the Baquerras, who overrun the small town of Arrey. The adobe warren of a house where Angel and his wife, Yvette, live is attached to a kind of general store—selling *piñatas*, soda pop, bait, sacks of dried pinto beans, gas, and oil—run by his sisters. His father, Angel, Sr., is selling wreaths of dried red peppers from a stand out front. His children are inside, watching *Aladdin*. All up and down the dirt roads of the county are free standing ovens, known as dehydration tunnels, where Baquerra relatives, on loan from Old Mexico, are drying Baquerra chile and packing them into boxes. Outside, migrant workers pick Baquerra chile.

It is clear that Angel, now thirty-two, is the reigning Baquerra of this empire. There is a lot of supervising to be done, and Angel's doing it, but he is not above stopping the car in the middle of a county road just to look at the sky. We lean against the truck for a while, sharing a bottle of water. The truck's mudflaps are decorated with the silhouette of a naked woman and the name "Lizette" in script. In his high-heeled underslung cowboy boots, jeans, diamond-snap western shirt, and straw cowboy hat, Angel looks like any other farmer in these parts—with a degree of added flash. He has told me that he is a brand-new born-again Christian, that he is dedicated first to God, then to his family, and then to the family business.

We are speeding along over ruts, through drifts of the small swallows Angel calls *golondrinas*, when Angel screeches to a stop and squats down beside a field of Joe Parker chile.

"Wilt rot," he pronounces. The peppers, which are about halfway from turning from green to red, are shriveled, almost as if by sun-drying. "They can't seem to find a seed resistant to this," Angel says. "That's why you see so much alfalfa around. Every three, four years they have to give it a rest. I guess it's time. Meanwhile, I guess we can grind 'em up."

Back at one of the Baquerra tunnels, he takes this up with a foreman, who, he suspects, but is not entirely sure, is a distant relative from El Charco de Peña, Chihuahua. As the cousins talk, *picante* wafts of chile scent from the big ovens blow toward us, causing my eyes to water and a helpless cough to linger in my throat. I stand there, weeping and hacking, while the two Baquerras ignore me politely, as do the ten or so elementary school–age children who are not in school but working right alongside their parents, doing jobs Baquerra deems totally beneath his own small boys. ("God no," he's said, "it's too hard. They love tractors, but I kind of hope they won't want to grow chile.")

It's different for Mexican nationals, he says, even if they are Baquerra relatives. The U.S. government is a little too easy on them, he thinks, with all the assistance it offers. "We grew up with the idea, all our lives, that there was some dignity to manual labor," he says. "Yeah, it was hard, but you just had to manage."

The prime example of this was Angel, Sr., born in 1935 in Julimas, Chihuahua. "I don't know the exact year he came over," Angel says, "but he came up and did anything involved with farming at all."

Within five years, Angel, Sr., had become a citizen and was sharecropping two different farms. "Then my mom came over, first working as a maid, and that lady helped her get her papers," Angel says. "They got married, and my mom and dad would work the fields all day and then my dad would go up to Albuquerque to sell the chile. He bought a three-room house and added on seven more rooms, one at a time, working sundown to midnight, every night."

By the time Angel was five, his father had a hundred acres planted with chile, and all four of his brothers and sisters were expected to help. Angel did, and he made it through high school and into the United

Technical Institute where he decided to get certified as an auto mechanic.

"One of my cousins and I went all the way to Phoenix for that school," Angel recalls. "My dad sent me away with a pickup load of powdered chile. He told me I could sell it to restaurants. I stayed eight months and lived off that chile the whole time."

Arizona farmers grow chile, but anywhere you go, there's a market for the peppers from Hatch. "I'm lucky we're famous," Angel admits. "The altitude up here, the cold winters, the mild summers—it all produces a certain flavor. If you were to bring in chile from Mexico and try to pass it off as Hatch chile, you wouldn't fool anyone."

Angel didn't last long as a mechanic. Soon he was back home, seeding *chile arbol* directly into the soil in March, going to Albuquerque to roast, dealing with guys like Charles Gurule, and doing the chile business exactly as his father had taught him. In those days, he says, chiles were dried by the sun, "laid out on the ground, or on a roof, like the Indians did. It gives it the most perfect sun-dried taste."

It was Angel who decided the Baquerras needed dehydration tunnels, "and we built three," he says. "The biggest guys around here have ten or twelve, but we did three and we're doing fine."

Right now the tunnels are holding steady at 150 degrees, and my sneezing and crying are worse than ever. "The people who work here, they just get used to it," Angel shrugs. "I'm used to it, too, unless you accidentally break a ripe chile and the juices get on you. No one *ever* gets used to that."

Then Angel climbs right into the oven alongside a box of chile that is slowly being drawn in on a conveyor belt. During the chile season, he'll often check the dehydrating process this way five or six times a day, even if he has to wake up in the middle of the night to do it. When he returns to the truck, he has barely broken a sweat, but it's hard work— exactly the kind that keeps away evil. Angel leans on the truck, looks off into the sky, and confronts the subject.

"You wouldn't think they had drugs in a rural place like this, would you?" he asks. "Well, they do, even cocaine, believe me." He remembers his youth as a wild haze of drinking, drugs, and whatever work he could manage. He remembers crying uncontrollably at the funeral of his younger brother, killed in a drunk driving accident, and going back out to get wasted that same night. Marriage to Yvette changed nothing.

"Our first seven years of marriage worked like this: she was married and I wasn't," he explains. "I made it a macho thing. She wasn't allowed to do much."

The rest of this revelation takes place back at the house, in a room with Yvette, a beautiful twenty-six-year-old woman with silky black hair down her back. Her face is so clean and clear she could pass for sixteen. She says she has her faith to thank. "The Lord found me when I was thirteen," she explains. "I started going to church meetings with my stepfather, which is lucky, because growing up in El Paso, I probably would have been a prostitute otherwise."

"Yeah, one time she brought over her preacher and I laughed in his face," Angel recalls. "I stayed drunk. And then one day, about six months ago, I saw that God's a big God. I asked Him, please, just *show me*. I didn't want no more cravings. And He did. I thought I was the only one who had ever been saved for a while. I started to witness God everywhere I went. But now I find I'm directed to people who want to hear about it. The rest of you," he says, looking at me with quiet intuition, "that's between you and God. What he wants for you. Looking at you, I can't tell."

"Hey," Yvette asks, "are you hungry at all?"

In fact, I have seldom been hungrier—having breathed in the heady, sneezy aroma of roasted chile all day, and run around at Angel's pace without so much as a taco between me and last night.

"Well, come here," she says proudly, flinging open her freezer door. Inside is an excellent selection of food from the Safeway freezer: pot pies, frozen pizza, Mrs. Paul's fish sticks, chicken nuggets. "You can have anything you want," she says.

I decide, somewhat rudely, to head for El Paso instead.

In actuality, I make it just to Anthony, a small town thirty miles from the Mexican border. In between a pawn shop and a wild roadhouse of a bar I find a small Mexican place. I order the chicken enchiladas smothered in red chili. "You use Hatch chile here?" I ask the man behind the counter.

"Of course."

My food arrives on a paper plate with a plastic fork. The smell of it rivals anything wonderful I have ever whiffed—a breath of ocean, an old rose, a lilac bush in bloom in a light rain. It makes me wonder why perfume counters in department stores take such pains to flood the air with what smells like bug spray. They could instead, I think, perfume their particular sky with Hatch chile. Then I begin to eat.

"I used to be a truck driver," the man behind the counter says, without prompting. "But I stay home now to be with my four-year-old son. I make my own tortillas, too."

"Didn't you like the open road?" I ask, with my mouth full.

"Yes, but love is more important than some things," he says.

I finish my enchiladas and beer, pay up, and drive southwest, into summer.

What to Do
❦ with Roasted Green Chile ❧

According to J. R. Perez: *Get you a pork chop and mix a salsa with tomatoes and green chile and fry it all up together, and that's the best thing you could ever have.*

Albert Perez: *Put your salsa over eggs and steak. Use yellow peppers when you want a change.*

Marcelline Perez: *When you have a sore throat, boil you some green chile and eat it with a spoon.*

Sam Arnold: *Make a Gonzales Steak. Chop up six Anaheim chile medium fine. In a small saucepan, heat one tablespoon of canola oil. Add one tablespoon of flour and cook into a roux. Add a half cup of chicken stock, some minced garlic and oregano, and cook until thick. Then add the chile. Cut a deep horizontal pocket in each of two top sirloin or New York strip steaks. Stuff each steak with some of the chile. Broil the steaks until medium rare.*

Willy Martinez: *You can have your green chile on a hamburger if you want. But me, I just eat it straight.*

3 Winter:
Bugs and Seeds

*Planning the garden takes place, as all
the handbooks advise, long before the
frost is out of the ground, preferably on a
night…with hail lashing the windows. The
dependents reverently produce the latest
seed catalogue and succumb to mass
hypnosis. "Look at these radishes—two
feet long!" everyone marvels. . . . A list of
staples is speedily drawn up: Brussels
sprouts the size of a rugby . . . let's have
plenty of beets, we can make our own
lump sugar. Then someone discovers the
hybrids—the onion crossed with a pepper
or a new vanilla-flavored turnip that plays
the "St. James Infirmary Blues." When the
envelope is finally sealed, the savings
account is a whited sepulchre and all we
need is a forty-mule team to haul the order
from the depot.*

S. J. PERELMAN, ACRES AND PAINS

Five dogs bark. I park in front of a beautiful,
run-down farm. It is February, but I am in northern California, and the
hillsides are green. It is getting on toward the rainy season, with plenty
of mud. I walk toward a dilapidated one-room house with a combination of yelling and music pouring out of it. Trim hangs from the eaves
and the porch is full of holes. How disreputable. Good. I'm here on a
disreputable errand.

I knock at the screen door. A tall man in baggy khakis answers.
He has tangled shoulder-length brown hair and a gap-toothed smile. I
realize that he is listening to a Sunday evangelical broadcast, complete
with rock band and choir.

"Yo!" the man says.

"Are you Exotic Botanicals of the Jungle?" I ask him.

"Nope," he answers. "They used to be here. They're gone."

"Where'd they go?"

"Oh, somewhere around here."

I explain that I have come from 1,500 miles away.

"You might try down Fratti Lane," the man suggests.

I drive back into Sebastopol—a town as cluttered with crystal mer-
chants as with 7-11s—and begin combing the woods for the producers
of the Exotic Botanicals of the Jungle plant and seed catalog. Not that
I mind the effort. It is far and away the most interesting thing I have
read this winter.

A small, black-and-white booklet with grainy photographs of
shamans and a few line drawings, Exotic Botanicals offers a selection
of plants and seeds from all over the world—and with a unique per-
spective. Have you ever read intros like "During a recent expedition
into the Oaxacan sierra to visit with Zapotec mushroom healer friends,
we . . . " or "Hottentot tribes smoke the sticky aromatic leaves &
flowertops as a preferred euphoriant . . . " in Burpee's? No one's name
appears anywhere in the catalog, nor does a street address, but it still

blooms with personal details. Like this:

Brunfelsia lactea

Endangered species from cloudforests of Jamaica's Blue Mountains. Reminiscent of vanilla and clove. We have kept several in 1-gallon pots, rotating the ones in bloom into the bedroom for pleasure-making. treelet $15

There is quite a bit of pleasure-making going on in this catalog: "Slowly chewing a matchstick-sized piece of gold root creates an intense tingling sensation on the lips and mouth. Experiments with the pleasant but dramatic skin tingling led us to use it erotically, as the sensation can be shared from the mouth onto other skin areas . . . use your imagination!"

And there are more kicks to be had. Offered for sale are Kola Nut Powder, which reportedly delivers "a full-on, one-by-one opening of the chakras as a kundalini-like mobilization of the vital forces." Or Kava Extract in liquid drops, an excellent "electroshock therapy pretreatment, proven to reduce mental disorganization at a cellular level. We do hope you never need to use it this way," the catalog adds kindly.

My copy, which was two years old when I obtained it third-hand, is packed with mail-order seeds and plants whose side effects are allegedly similar to cannabis, cocaine, heroin, and other recreational drugs. Lest anyone get the wrong idea, however, a stern disclaimer appears on the first page.

"The propagule units listed here are intended for cultivation as houseplants only," it reads. "The data provided on folk uses is given for historical interest and can be found in ethnobotanical literature. We do not suggest or imply attempting such folk use, nor guarantee any such claims regarding medicinal or other attributes to be correct. . . . We accept no responsibility for the outcome of use or misuse of anything we offer. Placing an order constitutes agreement to these terms."

I finally locate Fratti Lane and, soon after, a redwood house with rainbow flags, a greenhouse, and solar panels. The door is answered by a state-of-the-art counterculture woman in what looks like a nightie. I hope I haven't interrupted anyone's pleasure-making. She doesn't look happy to see me, and says she is *not* Exotic Botanicals, nor has she ever heard of them.

"Rats," I say, "I've come a long way, and they don't even have a phone number, and—"

"Maybe," she suggests, "it's because they don't want anyone calling them up."

"Do you think you might remember who they are after I leave?" I ask.

"Probably," she says evenly.

"Well, give them my card," I say. "Ask them to call."

"Okay."

"You sure you can't remember while I'm here?"

"I'm sure."

She blocks the door, but I can see enough. The place is packed with plants, from floor to ceiling. For all I know they are Hawaiian wood rose, gold root, and *Brunfelsia lactea*.

"Try to get them to call me, okay?"

Of course, they never do. But that's okay. I'm not usually this entertained in midwinter.

⚘ ☀ ⚘

I don't put my garden to bed. It's not because I haven't read the articles. I've seen the pictures of newly oiled spade handles and raised beds covered in straw. I even take a sort of detached pleasure in all that. I just don't do it.

Instead, I let the garden wither away on its own. I don't go out and look at it, either—frostbitten tomatoes turned hollow and brown are not a pretty sight. And what good would it do to stare at seed heads stuck to stalks or a rusty rake with tongs pointing dangerously up? I let the beans dry on the vine. I hate winter. I don't care. Worms, rot, working compost, roots cruising into the earth—these are what make life interesting. In winter, life isn't interesting unless you have a thing for ice.

Or unless you are walking through ice, in winter, to get at something live and deliberately related to gardening, which is what interests me about Doug Beck. Beck is the president of a company called the California Garden Ladies, which provides sacks of live ladybugs to catalog wholesalers, as well as to retail outlets as far away as Colorado.

"Is it true that you breed ladybugs in captivity?" I asked him on the phone a few weeks ago.

"Are you kidding?" he answered. "No one does that. No one can. A ladybug won't do that."

"What about the California Garden Ladies? Is it true they're the first all-female bug collective?"

55

"The Ladies," he explained patiently, "are the bugs. *Lady*bugs."

"So it's just you and a bunch of bugs?"

"Yeah," he said, "plus a couple of my brothers and a cousin and an uncle, part time. Bugging kind of runs in the family. If you come up here," he added, "I'll show you a picture of myself completely covered with ten thousand beetles. Crusted all over my face and everything."

This is all I needed to hear. Beck lives a few miles outside the town of Grass Valley, in the Sierra Nevada, known as Mother Lode Country—once because of the California Gold Rush, but now because of ladybugs. Ladybugs have been a staple of gardening catalogs for more than fifty years, especially whenever chemical insecticides fall out of favor. This is because ladybugs eat aphids and other unwelcome, soft-bodied bugs. The variable is: Once imported to your garden, will they stay there, or fly away home? No scientist has ever come up with the answer to this, but ladybugs seem to work well enough in home gardens to assume the importance of a cash crop.

"You could always sell them," Beck tells me as we sit at his kitchen table putting off going out into the snow. "I remember riding my bicycle after them when I was a kid. You could make good chewing-gum money just from selling ladybugs."

But it was hardly a living. Beck's father and mother did some logging, the five children did some bugging, and they all hated time clocks, which sometimes led his father into side ventures. One year, he built a forty-five-foot salmon trawler in the backyard and promptly got lost for a week near Hawaii. To this day, during the off season, Beck still does a little logging, when he's not engaged in such freelance pursuits as building waterfalls or flying his ultralight airplane over the rice fields to scare away blackbirds.

It has only been over the past two years, Beck says, that he has taken the bug business seriously, signing a contract with a southern California distributor to bring in two-thousand gallons of ladybugs each year, and increasing his retail business to another thousand gallons. For the first time in his thirty-four years, even though he continues to clean and ship bugs from his backyard, he is seen around town as something of a mogul.

"Yeah, and I hate people," he says. "They ask what I'm doing, and for what it's worth, I lie and say I'm barely getting by. What would *you* say—there's a gold mine up the road, help yourself?"

It is mid-February, and the gold mine is about to reopen for the season. The ladies are bored with hibernation. "We'll see them boiling up around the base of the trees, if the afternoon sun heats up," he says, but he continues to sit somewhat defeatedly at the kitchen table, staring at a wilted Valentine's Day flower arrangement.

"Women," he offers. "It's a long, long story. . . . " He pauses, then finally says, "Let's get down to bugs. Summer bugs are different than winter bugs, you know. Here it is winter, and this snow, if you want to know, concerns me."

We go out to a small economy car, and begin loading it with the tools of the trade—a Homelite chainsaw, pigskin gloves, several plastic kitty-litter trays, and burlap sacks. Sometimes, during the summer, Beck will drive four hundred miles in a southwestern loop, from the Sierra Nevada down into Yosemite, looking for bug beds, and not necessarily finding them. He will walk stream beds for hours, drive his all-terrain vehicle deep into the woods, or, when he finds a likely looking brushfall, attack it with a shovel or chainsaw. Several times in a season, he'll come home covered with poison oak, or snakebit. And through all those miles, his thoughts seldom stray from the subject of ladybugs.

There are thousands of different kinds of ladybugs, he tells me, and they come in a huge selection of colors, from red with black spots, to black with red spots, to all black, to all red, to all yellow. The bug we're looking for, though, is known as *Hippodamia convergens*, and it generally—though not always—comes in the basic ladybug color combination. It is famous for having saved the entire California citrus crop in 1888 by eating its cottony-cushion scale bug attackers. It is also noted for its unusually predictable migration patterns, which are most obvious in and around the Sierra Nevada, even though *H. convergens* can be found all over the United States.

In brief, *H. convergens'* approximate one year of life works like this. The female ladybug lays her eggs in mid-spring in Sacramento's Central Valley, after having gorged herself on aphids. The new bugs emerge as larvae, looking not at all like the cheerful Volkswagen bug you might expect, but more like vicious worms with pointy heads, six foreshortened legs, and no wings. During the next five weeks or so, the larval beetles become very active predators, eating up to one thousand aphids apiece. They then retreat to a pupal case—which, unlike the caterpillar's spun-silk cocoon, actually consists of the larval beetle's own exoskeleton. After about a week, they emerge as adult beetles, complete with two sets of shell-like wings, the expected markings, and their hunger intact. But by this time—late spring—there are few aphids left to eat, so they migrate up to the higher, cooler Sierra Nevada, where they eat the pollen of alpine flowers, storing it as body fat, which looks not unlike our own yellow globules of insulation.

In the Sierra Nevada, *H. convergens* spend the summer in estivation, a sort of warm-weather hibernation during which they live off the stored body fat until the colder autumn weather wakes them just long enough to relocate to a reliably warm spot—perhaps the south side of a tree that receives afternoon sun. There, they bed down beneath layers of leaves, by the hundreds of thousands, until the urge to mate wakes them again in early spring. After mating, they fly back down to the Central Valley, eat lots of aphids, and die.

There are hundreds of variations on this theme. Not all ladybird beetles live for exactly one year, and some lay eggs more than once before they die. In other parts of the country, their migration follows a completely different pattern. But this is the basic scenario Beck keeps in mind as he looks for bugs.

"To find a bug," Beck says, "you really have to have the mind of a bug. You just can't cover ground. You have to find where they would have been hibernating since last June and find them on a warm afternoon when they're getting ready to fly. You look for veins of red over in the leaves."

We've been driving down a national forest access road for the past fifteen minutes. Now Beck pulls over, gets out, and loads up with sacks and pans. We begin to walk in a way that seems random to me—no straight lines or marked paths. In the distance, I can hear a roaring creek. Beck is looking for an ideal situation: big trees at the edge of a clearing, where afternoon sun can warm the mulch at the base of the trunks. After a half hour, he finds just such a place—and in this case even I can see the red veins among the leaves. Putting on his gloves, Beck begins to rummage through a foot-deep layer of composted leaves, twigs, and dirt. Less than an inch down, he hits stratum after stratum of ladybugs. The bugs are slow-moving and a little annoyed, but those that are mating when we find them continue to do so.

"It's almost impossible to tell which are male and which are female," Beck observes. "I don't even think the ladybugs know until they try. They also eat each other. They get in your face, crawl in your eyes, ears, and nose. Plus, they'll bite the crap outta you."

It feels like a mild nip, Beck says, and he doesn't know why they do it. Today, they remain docile as he shovels them by the handful into his pan, shaking it so they fall to the bottom, then stuffing them into a sack. It looks to me as if he has caught several million bugs.

"Nah," Beck says. "That's maybe a gallon. My brother Dusty and I did a hundred and seventy-six gallons one day last fall." Not today. The snow, which fell late in the year for these parts, has made the bugs less willing to fly. If they won't fly, we'll have trouble seeing them. The minute the weather warms up, even by a couple of degrees, the bug beds will be much more obvious, and Beck will be well on his way to the seasonal goal of three thousand gallons. "I may need a couple of my brothers to help me," he says. "By summer, I'll be out there every day, going down cliffs after them, going into the brambles with my chainsaw. I'll stop every couple hours to wet them down so they don't cook to death."

There is a furtive sound to Beck's voice, and I realize he is deliberately trying not to make much noise. It would be just as well, he says, if no one knew we were here. You don't need a license to hunt bugs, and we're currently hunting in a national forest, but many bugging grounds in these parts are held by unofficial family leases, sometimes for generations. Bug hunters are a secretive lot. They do not go out of their way to run into each other.

"One time I was hiking out of a canyon with a couple of incriminating-looking sacks," Beck recalls, "and I had a guy stick a gun right in my face and he said: 'What the hell are you doing here?' It's hard to say anything with a gun in your face, even the truth." Another well-known bug baron in her sixties has threatened Beck specifically and repeatedly. "She said she'd kill me if she ever found me in one of her beds," he says.

Back at home with a carload of ladybugs, Beck will unload the sacks onto a screened platform and shake chalk on top of the piles. Ladybugs don't like chalk, and they walk away from the debris into mesh sacks filled with fine wood shavings, which Beck then ships by refrigerated freight to his retail outlets. (I have seen his displays, and heard them hissing at the checkout line of my local garden store. What I like best about them is their seemingly hand-drawn labels, featuring "1,500 California Showbugs" and a drawing of a puny aphid being terrorized by ladybugs sporting top hats and canes. What I like least about them is the fact that the ladybugs' legs sometimes get caught in the mesh and snap off.) Beck has spent many a long hour separating bugs for shipping and contemplating their unique problems, the most alarming of which is, of course, their propensity to fly away.

"I've tried making up a sort of sugar water," Beck says. "You spray it on them and their wings stick together. But only for a while. And my mom keeps trying to invent a tunnel, where the bugs see a light and walk toward it, and a tiny brush comes down and paints their wings with glue. Doesn't work yet, though. The bugs always try to climb up the paintbrush."

The bugs are nearly impossible to domesticate. They don't go to work—eating aphids and laying eggs—unless they feel like it. If they don't like your garden, they won't stick around. I admire their independence.

"Me, too," Beck agrees. "You can get burned out with bugs, but never bored."

ᏨᏳᎾ

From the Arbico catalog of Tucson, Arizona:

Ladybird Beetle

The most common of all beneficial insects, these voracious predators not only rid the garden and greenhouse of pests, but are cost effective as well.... During the larval stage, the ladybug resembles a tiny, black, six-legged alligator with orange spots. It will gorge on approximately 400 aphids. After 4 or 5 weeks it attaches itself to leaves and twigs in order to enter the pupal phase of development. After one week, the pupal casing bursts open and the famished young adult emerges. An adult ladybug will consume approximately 5,000 additional aphids. In a few weeks, tiny yellow eggs will be deposited. Several generations may be produced. $8.50 per pound.

I don't need the Arbico people's ladybugs—not when I know their source—but that has not stopped them from clogging my mailbox with solicitations to buy. Ever since the first of the year, catalogs have been piling up in drifts. I could not possibly patronize them all. And yet, they all seem to have my number:

Because you're a Spring Hill Preferred Customer, <u>ROBIN CHOTZINOFF</u>, we'd like to send you a very special FREE gift . . . two beautiful Stella De Oro Dwarf Daylilies to plant in the <u>Chotzinoff Garden</u> . . . guaranteed to grow and bloom in <u>Denver County, Colorado</u> . . . around the <u>Chotzinoff</u> home.

There is more, having to do with what the <u>Chotzinoff</u> neighbors— entirely silent up till now—will say when they see my yard this summer. Pretty soon I am deep in the well-organized, color-coordinated world of Spring Hill Gardens, with its Red Garden, Pink Garden, Easy-Care Shade Garden, Lifetime Peony Garden—oh, and the Freedom Hedge Rose. "People keep knocking at my door wondering if they are plastic," writes dentist Kevin Osborn of Houston Heights. "Thank you for the beauty!"

Before I can commit to Spring Hill, though, I notice the Breck's of Holland catalog leering at me from the coffee table.

"Ordering Breck's bulbs for the Chotzinoff garden is just like having your own personal buying agent in Holland," I read. And what an agent! Breck's is celebrating its four-hundredth anniversary in the bulb business, and knows whereof it speaks. I spend an interesting interlude with the history of the tulip, which was brought to Vienna from Asia Minor by an emissary of Austrian emperor Ferdinand I. "The handful of bulbs first bloomed in the spring of 1594," I read, "and they caused a sensation."

Well, so will the Rembrandt tulips and Siberian iris I now must have. But then how will I afford a riding tractor with a chipper/shredder attachment, which I covet, even though I don't own a rugged hillside covered with brambles and brush?

A Victorian gazing ball from hoity-toity Jackson & Perkins would be more appropriate, but if I had fifty dollars, I'd spend it all on the *All Blue Potato!*, which the Gurney's catalog calls "deliciously different! Play the blues and get everyone's attention!" Gurney's manages to give the impression that gardening is not a solitary, meditative pursuit so much as something we do to knock each other's socks off.

"My friends have never seen such a BIG sweet potato!" writes one Charles Grazevich of Augusta, New Jersey. "It weighed in at $6^1/2$ pounds and measured twelve inches long and 15 inches wide. I grew it during a mild, rainy summer," he adds, by way of anticlimax.

Perhaps I'll order the giant Carolina Cross watermelon, with its two-hundred-pound fruits. "You'll be able to bring dessert no matter how big the family picnic," Gurney's enthuses. A few pages later, though, the dangers of such megacrops become clear.

"Please be careful how you advertise your seeds!" writes Dr. Willis G. Dick of Iola, Kansas. "These banana squash were said to grow 10–12 pounds. This one measured $34^1/2$ inches from tail to nose and weighed 38 pounds!" How can I live without one? Also—a squeezer/strainer, a grain grinder, cherry stoner, and bean frencher.

A newsletter from the Center for Historic Plants at Thomas Jefferson's

Monticello is not as breathless with excitement, but has its moments. I note, right away, that Thomas Jefferson and I have exactly the same taste in flowers: nasturtium, larkspur, four o' clock, Nora Barlow columbine, and Canterbury bells are all in my garden as well as his. Jefferson thought the scarlet runner bean visually "delicious." I agree.

Historian Gary Wills, parts of whose lecture on Jefferson are reprinted in the catalog, loves him for doing "what all good gardeners do. When he realized he couldn't take care of a small garden," Wills writes, "he made it three times larger."

This year's Rocky Mountain Seed Company catalog is almost as historic as Monticello, in that it hasn't changed a whit in seventy-four years. The same rooster spreads its wings on the cover, and the same no-nonsense paragraphs run throughout, describing crops like mountain brome and sheep fescue. It's not a place for the foo-foo home gardener. So frill-less is this oeuvre that its most riveting prose comes in a section devoted not to seeds or implements but to the rubber bands truck gardeners use to assemble carrots and greens into bunches.

"Made with electronic control," the catalog says sparingly, "to give improved stretch, smoother and higher count per pound. Used by vegetable growers around the world."

But the Chotzinoff garden does not need rubber bands. What it needs, I conclude, after a winter's worth of armchair catalog leafing, is a beautifully tangled mess of flowering vines, rare herbs, old-fashioned flowers, and little-known European vegetables—the very nucleus of the Shepherd's catalog. It's been my favorite for nearly ten years.

Unlike the faceless voices of the big chain catalogs—Earl May, A. R. Gurney, W. Atlee Burpee, and Henry Field have been dead for decades—Shepherd's is the vision of an actual person. Renee Shepherd is a relative newcomer, having been in seeds just over ten years, but her catalog is a refreshment. Who else would write of winter squash that "having a good supply will make you feel both wise and self-reliant"? Who else would confess to gaining weight on every European seed-buying trip? Who else prints a recipe on every page?

Reading through the Shepherd's catalog inspires in me more than the simple urge to spend a lot of money and overplant. It makes me want to coddle something precious and unusual, like a Baby Boo minipumpkin or a crop of Dutch carrots with the nice Puerto Rican name of Caramba. If I did, it wouldn't be just for show, either. Every seed in this catalog is picked for taste—the very reason Renee Shepherd started the company.

Bigger seed outfits, she noticed, had failed to take advantage of lesser-known European seeds, bred more for flavor than ease of shipping. Her approach coincided nicely with the culinary boom of the late eighties and early nineties, and the company's done well. In 1987, Renee Shepherd sold her company to Eliot Wadsworth, a Connecticut entrepreneur who also owns White Flower Farm. But she hung on to artistic and editorial control, and as far as the catalog is concerned, nothing has changed. It retains the feel of a small, intimate outfit, where people are always harvesting or eating something.

"Well, we do invite you to be in touch," says Wendy Krupnick, the voice who answers the phone at the Shepherd's office in Felton, California, ten miles north of Santa Cruz. "Our emphasis since the beginning has been on lots of horticultural advice. I mean, we did start out selling things no one knows how to grow, like radicchio and fennel. We have to help you a little, or what's the point?"

Sometimes it comes down to conversation. Like me, a lot of the Shepherd's callers are winter-bound, with dreams of spring they can't seem to shake. "I just got off the phone with a woman from California who was stuck in an ice storm in North Carolina," Wendy says. "As far as I can tell, she called because she's frustrated."

At the end of February, I decide to visit. Beth Benjamin, Renee Shepherd's right-hand woman, handles my request. "You're one of those people in a cold place," she says. "We get a lot of calls from those cold places, especially Minnesota. It feels like they just want to keep you on the phone when the snow begins to fly."

The climate around Felton sometimes turns rainy in winter, but frost is rare, she says. The Shepherd's staff is busy inside because mail orders are beginning to pile up. In other words, Beth says, where she is, spring has already begun.

Outside my window, in Denver, a layer of gray, polluted air presses against the mountains. I hang up the phone, and within a week, I am sitting with Beth in the small, seed-crammed nook she calls "our palatial conference room." Like the rest of the three-room office, it is unpretentious and temporary-looking. The whole entity occupies a small part of a rural strip mall. The atmosphere here is comfortable and maternal—one employee carries a newborn baby on her back as she works, and everyone's eating cake. Beth herself is large, friendly, and unhampered by makeup, a hairbrush, or fashion. That she and Shepherd's look alike is no accident—she's worked here, first in a number of part-time jobs and now as full-time office manager, since the business began in Renee Shepherd's spare bedroom in 1982.

"I belong here, I suppose," she says. "I was always around gardens growing up. I learned to garden with my grandmother in the first place, but I had sixty-seven unspecific hopes and desires by the time I left home. I seem to remember wanting to be a writer or go into the foreign service."

She ended up at the University of California at Santa Cruz in the early sixties, where she came under the spell of a British gardener named Alan Chadwick.

"He was very lordly and very impatient," she recalls. "He was this blueblood, real tan, lean, and muscular, always dressed nautically. He was the second son of a wealthy British family, a real mythological character. People were trying to do biographies of him while he was still alive. He'd been a musician, an actor, a dancer—but his family looked upon him as a black sheep."

So Chadwick gravitated to Santa Cruz and dug out a five-acre garden located on a steep and brushy hillside where college policy, until then, had been to simply cut down the weeds. His first garden tended toward the formal and British, with perennial borders and neat pathways. Students like Beth, for lack of anything more interesting to do, helped him with the planting and weeding. It was unlike any menial work Beth had ever done before.

"Alan was so enlightened as to the forces that were going on behind those dull chores," she remembers. "Soon the university began trying to kick us off, but a lot of people came and everyone did a little. We started growing flowers for love, fun, and practice. We put them in a kiosk and gave them away to anyone who wanted them. We stayed and became outlaw gardeners."

Beth dropped out of school to garden full time, and when she married, she and her (now ex-) husband started Camp Joy, a four-acre farm near Felton where they intended to teach gardening and grow organic vegetables. It was Chadwick's example—even though he could be authoritarian and brisk—that showed them the way. "The whole thing of gardening as a way of life," Beth says. "Alan started all that—not just here, but all across the country. I presume there are places where no one cares about fresh food, but I can't understand it. A well-grown carrot is just not the same as a dead supermarket carrot."

Upon leaving Camp Joy in the early eighties, Beth began writing seed packet copy for Renee Shepherd. It turned out the two shared an obsession with food. "Renee and I used to go to every seed trial we could find," Beth recalls. "We'd spend days tasting broccoli and tomatoes. We were two women in a sea of commercial broccoli buyers, who were all men, and these broccoli guys wanted real different things, like ease of shipping and the ability to predict a specific harvest. We, on the other hand, wanted plants that would produce side shoots and a wonderful taste. They'd just *look* at us."

No longer. With three million copies of the Shepherd's catalog in circulation, and Renee Shepherd spending at least half her time searching out seeds, Beth has been left with a big, successful business to run. It would be satisfying, she says, if there were any time left to garden.

"There's so much new to grow," she says, a little wistfully. "Like the new arugula. It's deeply cut, beautiful. Renee ate it in Italy and had to have it. There's this tomato, Big Beef, and a whole bunch of new basils, Thai basil, a little red leaf basil from Holland, and a *red* habañero chili. Also flowering vines and Lavender Lady, a lavender you can really start from seed."

Beth gives me a packet to take home. (It germinates, but I neglect it to death a few months later.) "I wish I could grow it myself," she says. "And I hate going to the store to buy vegetables. I should never have to go to the store. All this talk about agribusiness, all that means to me is my own backyard."

❦ ☀ ❦

The trip to California changes my view of winter. What goes on in winter is not nothing, I decide, but a sort of holing up. I begin to hoard seed packets, spreading them out on my dining room table and remembering pregnancy. For nearly ten months, all the energy I could produce was diverted into something unknown. Nurturing thoughts did not sustain me through that time—in fact, if there is a nurturing bone in my body, I have yet to locate it. What kept me going was the possibility of a future adventure. And I was right—the adventure has barely stopped since my daughter, Coco, was born six years ago. Sometimes when I look at her, I think: all that, from a seed. An innocuous pellet, big as a BB or fine as dust. A seed is something to pay attention to in winter.

65

Rick Roen is a selfish gardener. He owns his own seed company. Every seed in the Lake Valley Seed Company is *his*.

"I just don't like business partners," he says. "I tried them and I don't like them. Luckily, the seed business is still very small and intuitive. No," he says into the phone, "lemon balm is almost impossible to get this year. I can't help you. Microclimates," he explains as he hangs up, "microclimates are why seeds are an international market. If you can grow one particular thing in your particular climate, you can offer it to the rest of the world. But one season of bad weather, and everything disappears. Flowering sweet peas, for instance."

There is a brief moment of regret for flowering sweet peas, but it passes. Traveling the world in the past year, Rick has found other flowers to love. "A scented class of phlox I found in Czechoslovakia," he offers. "During the day it looks like some kind of obscure weed, but at night it has this powerful fragrance." A chocolate columbine whose scent alone makes it worthwhile. Rick shows me the seed packet. "It's a crummy picture," he admits, "but it's a crummy-looking flower. That's not the point, anyway."

Rick's small office, tacked onto a warehouse in Boulder, Colorado, is crammed with dried flowers in distinctly manly arrangements. Three-foot-high spikes of blue oregano flowers, for instance, jammed into a ceramic pot, and tottering slightly. Rick is a big, blond, handsome man—definitely a hippy turned entrepreneur. He is wearing his daily uniform of jeans and a seed company T-shirt. On his desk in no particular order are: a package of sun-dried tomatoes, a golden railroad spike, hills of paper, Girl Scout cookies, and seed packet prototypes from the Vilmorin Seed Company, France. Although Rick is not immune to the trappings and language of success—he can talk venture capital until my eyes glaze over—a fancy office means nothing to him. Besides, he's not around that much, anyway.

"My job," he says, "is to go out and find stuff. Seeds. Anywhere between Europe and the West Coast. I know, it sounds adventurous, but a lot of it is just standing out in a field looking at plants. My wife always thinks she wants to go with me, because it's Europe. But could she *ever* spend the whole day in a field?"

It took a good twenty years for Rick to build up the required stamina. Growing up in Littleton, a suburb of Denver, he remembers not paying any particular attention to plants, other than the lawn he had to mow. As an electrical engineering student in Boulder in the early seventies, though, he became fascinated with natural food stores. "They were some of the first in the country," he recalls. "The one I went to work for sold bulk spices and herbs. We would mill down whole spices." While doing so, he'd wonder how far into the world you had to go to see where these exotic crops grew.

By 1975, Rick had dropped out of college and decided he wanted his own herb company, and as long as he was at it, he would carry herb seeds for gardeners. "The big catalogs just weren't paying that much attention to herbs back then," he explains. "Most of the big guys had no contact with people who grew herbs. It was just a little offshoot I was able to see."

A decade managing a publicly traded herb and seed company followed. By 1984, Rick had had enough of cooperation with a board of directors and decided just to own his own seed company.

"I thought I'd start up easy," he recalls. "My special niches were wild-flowers and herbs. But as chain stores became more dominant, the big seed companies began cutting out the interesting varieties. Places like Wal-Mart were taken over by Burpee and Northrup-King. And retail prices were raised thirty to forty percent to allow for a thirty- to forty-percent price cut."

It worked at Wal-Mart, he says, but not at small hardware stores and garden centers, which is why he decided to develop a moderately priced line of seeds with enough variety to keep any gardener interested.

His travels began. "I had to try Europe," he remembers. "They don't have to ship as far and they have a much richer culinary heritage. They might pay more attention to taste than quantity. I thought, Americans should discover these seeds."

Clearly, so did Renee Shepherd and Rob Johnston of Johnnie's Seeds in Albion, Maine. Rick says the three were aware of each other's businesses from the start, often share information, and are friends more than competitors. "The catalogs do better with those really exotic seeds, though," he says, and there is no Lake Valley Seed Company catalog, which means Rick must walk the fine line between newfangled (Triomphe de Farcy string beans) and old reliable (Heavenly Blue morning glories.)

"Finding seed is the fun part," he says. "In Holland, I go see this maniacal Dutch guy. He has fifteen acres planted in seed trials. With him, I'll stay up all night and all day in the field with restaurants and bars in between. He loves to entertain, to talk about plants. Here in the United States, going through a field of beans isn't so great, but the tomato trials in September are like a sixth-grade field trip for me. Last year I tasted two-hundred-and-fifty different varieties." In Belize last month, Rick visited a vegetable market and found the elusive red habañero chile—perhaps at the same time Renee Shepherd and Beth Benjamin were falling for it. Rick hasn't introduced it as a Lake Valley Seed yet, but he'll probably have it in his own garden. "I started that seed last week," he admits.

"Could I see your garden?" I ask.

"Maybe in the spring," he says. "Besides, I don't really want to share my garden, when you come right down to it. I have two fifty-by-one-hundred-foot plots, and my wife complains all the time that they're not pretty at all. It's just in rows, everything, my flowers, my vegetables. You should visit Johnnie's. Their garden is *much* nicer than mine. Most gardens are."

"It sounds like my garden," I say. "It doesn't look like much of anything. And by August it's full of weeds."

"And that's *okay*," Rick says heatedly. "People don't seem to understand that amending the soil and all that—you don't *have* to do that stuff. If by July, it's too hot to sow successive crops and you don't care anymore—that's *okay*. A lot of years in August, I look forward to the first frost. So what? I'm not even that into touring other people's gardens unless they're going to give me a plant or something."

"Me, too," I say. "So what *is* it about gardening?"

"It's a meditation," Rick says. "I don't think, necessarily, when I'm gardening. I have an active mind and I'm always talking, talking and thinking. In the garden, I'm not. I'm a much more relaxed gardener than anyone I know. I grow it for my own edification, and that's all."

"So what will you plant this year?" I ask.

"New things," he says. "New things are what I like."

We begin walking through the seed warehouse, in search of new things. "A seed company is a mixture of very modern and very anti-quated," he observes—correctly, as it turns out. A rather elaborate computer system manages the wholesale orders, but the seeds are still pulled by hand from shelves, and the equipment used to print seed packets seems a hundred years old. Canvas sacks and cardboard drums of bulk seed lean in the corners, giving off a faint smell of foreign lands.

"Cosmos," Rick says. "We have ten or eleven different kinds. Want some?"

"Not enough light," I say, regretfully.

"How about this nasturtium," he says, handing over a packet. "It's mahogany-colored. It's a love-hate flower. I don't care for it."

Pretty soon, I have an armload of free seed packets—some exotic, like East German amaranth, and some apple-pie American, like sweet alyssum, white.

"Common to obscure, that's what you have," Rick says. "I try to be universal. Morning glories, alyssum. Most of our sales are of common things. That's what people like. Gardeners are conservative."

"How can you say that?" I ask, almost running to keep up as he strides through aisles of seed.

"Well, millions of people out there grow Kentucky Wonder pole beans," he says. "There must be something good about them, don't you think?" He hands me an envelope full of bean seed.

Later that day, I add the pole beans to my hoard. Good old American beans. There *is* something good about the sight of them growing up a pole—or, in the case of my garden, an old pool cue. There is something even better about being just one of millions of people who will grow them—when the soil warms up, months from now. I sit down at the dining room table and begin to deal out my seeds like a pack of cards. One of the millions, waiting for spring.

4 City Dirt

. . . one could look forward to the week of Succoth, when my father would construct a shelter close to the row of toilets in the back yard and cover it with pine branches. Here we would have all our meals, even on cold days or when it rained. This was decidedly life in the open! Sitting at supper in the rustic hut, with the rain leaking through the prickly foliage, gave one a sense of communion with nature, and, indeed, of being a member of some close-knit, savage tribe.

SAMUEL CHOTZINOFF, A LOST PARADISE

I did not grow up in the presence of direct light.

We lived nine floors up in a very nice nine-room Manhattan apartment on the Upper West Side. The only way to see the sky was to open the window wide and stick your head out far enough to look straight up.

Growing things did not interest my family much, but that is not to say nothing grew. My stepfather had one Thai pepper plant that sat in the kitchen, which was painted yellow to give the impression of sun. And I do mean *impression*—the air we lived in was so full of cinders that when I took a yellow tennis ball up on the roof to hit, it turned black in less than ten minutes. Down on the street, small valiant trees grew from holes in the sidewalk, supported by what looked like rubber dog collars. Around them was the smell of the subway, hot dogs from a cart, and whatever lurks below the gratings where deliveries are made.

I learned the smell of vegetation during summers on eastern Long Island. Wandering through an abandoned lot where a house must once have been, I learned the stunning abundance of a backyard garden. The empty house foundations were alive with flowers—a blue hydrangea, a spirea covered with bees, fancy white roses gone wild. Rhubarb, lettuce, spinach, and mint grown to the size of hedges. With a little room, it seemed, you could produce jungles to play and forage in.

But despite the genteel circles in which I was raised, I don't remember that anyone had any room at all in New York City. Sometimes, in spring, I would smell wet leaves or cherry blossoms, as if blown in from another planet. Or there would be a bucket of forsythia on the sidewalk in front of a neighborhood grocery store. But you don't grow things in the city, I thought.

Fast forward. I am nineteen. I have spent the past two years barely attending college and working on grounds crews, planting azalea beds, digging weeds out from between bricks, ripping dead ivy from ivy-covered walls. Now I have given up, dropped out, and moved West. My first real boyfriend and I have just broken up. I am alone in a basement apartment with a tiny patch of hard-packed dirt—perhaps four square feet—outside the kitchen door. I have planted two six-packs of petunias there, and am posing for a picture. I send the picture to my mother. It's the only picture from that era she can stand to look at.

Nearly twenty years later, I realize that I've been gardening small, untalented, urban plots ever since that picture was taken. The only kind of garden I've ever had is a city garden. And the thing is, I like it. I like my inadequate gardening tools—the ridiculous folding camping shovel, the rusty clippers. I appreciate my latest and smallest yard with its yellowing lawn and elm beetles falling from the trees. I savor the hot weekend afternoons spent patrolling in my lucky garden clothes: weight belt, ancient skirted bathing suit, L. L. Bean duck-hunting boots. I like the busybody neighbors and their advice, the invasion of the morning glory and squash vines, the sound of loud Mexican pop music from a low-rider in the alley.

In Denver, urban atmosphere mixes painlessly with country sounds and smells. Under the gang graffiti on my fence, grasshoppers saw their wings together. My neighbors keep chickens and rabbits in their yards, in direct violation of city law. I know it is morning when someone's El Camino backfires as he leaves for work, but also when the cock crows.

Who am I kidding? This is no kind of city at all. In spring, when my family used to decamp to the country, I decide to do the opposite. I get on a plane and go back east in search of real urban gardens.

❧ ☀ ☙

In late April, with the azaleas blooming in almost man-made Technicolor, I stand in a Washington, D.C., backyard as small as my own. A group of well-meaning volunteers from the Georgetown Day School has been coming by all spring to help out, and now, says Sue Shankle, the social worker in charge, everything is in a shambles.

"Bless their little hearts," she says acidly. "They didn't know what was what. They stuck one gladiolus bulb in the middle of the yard, and ran around using lots of muscle power. The women who come here, they know more about gardening than those kids. Absolutely they know more."

But upscale high school students are drawn irresistibly to places like Rachael's Women's Center. As a charitable endeavor, it has everything: the homeless, the chronically mentally ill, survivors of abuse and battery, even a location in a scary neighborhood.

"It's a prostitution-type area," Sue explained to me on the phone. "So that's who all those women will be that you might see on your way down here. Don't give them a second thought."

Rachael's Women's Center is part of a block of modest row houses not far from downtown D.C. The house, an 1850s-era brownstone with an off-kilter staircase, high ceilings, and ornate plasterwork above ancient electrical sockets, has been made over as a drop-in day shelter for homeless women.

"Many of the night shelters close during the day," Sue explains. "During the day is when these women have to get their business taken care of. We provide a place where they can do that, and a place with no men. Many bring their babies."

On a normal day, Sue would be busy with her roster of fifteen mentally ill women, doing everything from helping them balance their checkbooks to trying to persuade them to take their antipsychotic medication, but today no one's home but her. A delegation of clients and staff has been dispatched to a city council meeting, where they will speak up for better and more available public housing.

"Which makes it a very D.C. kind of day for them," Sue says. "Not for me. I'm gonna just stay here and garden."

This is Sue's second year working the tiny back garden, where a few shrubs are blooming, tulips are just finishing, and the compost is beginning to heat up. By summer, it will be a riot of tomatoes, peppers, and cutting flowers—not to mention a pickling cucumber vine snaking nine feet up into a locust tree. The flowers and the food will end up on the tables where free lunch is served every weekday. But the true benefits of the garden will be more cerebral.

"The fruits of your labor, literally, you can eat them," Sue says, "but it's more. You can name those weeds when you pull them out. We're talking about mostly mentally ill women here, the sickest women of all. They're disorganized and scattered, and they come from all over the country so they can sue the government or the FBI. Gardening," she says, in her soft North Carolina accent, "gives them some time *not* to be paranoid."

Sue has the traditional social worker's arsenal on hand—medication, welfare programs, support groups, counseling—but gardening's worked for her, and that's what she pushes. "Talking therapy," she laughs, "it's for the worried well. For me, when I first came to the city, I had to realize I was born with dirt on my hands. I thought, 'I'm gon' get sick if

75

I don't grow something.'"

Sue is of the opinion that the lust for gardening skips a generation. It first came upon her in her grandmother's garden in Greensboro, North Carolina, home to just about all the Shankles she can name, half of whom were gardeners, and all of whom had consciences that wouldn't quit.

"I come from a long line of doctors, nurses, circuit riding preachers, and social workers," she says. "We were *never* slave owners. My dad was the only doctor in town who got paid in chickens. He would go out in the garden and pick an ear of corn to eat for breakfast."

As a teenager, Sue tended her grandmother's camellias because she was expected to, but what she really loved was the hill behind her grandmother's house, where more than a thousand daffodils bloomed.

"Two years ago in the spring, when my grandmother was dying, I went back home and picked every flower off that hillside," Sue recalls, "and I brought 'em to her hospital room. I kept thinking, she can't die till she's seen Mrs. Backhouse, which was her favorite daffodil. She almost died right in front of me, but then she sat up in bed and said, 'Mrs. Backhouse,' loud and clear."

Sue could have stayed in Greensboro with Mrs. Backhouse and her family garden, but six years ago, at the age of thirty-five, she came to D.C. "because sometimes it's time to go." She landed almost immediately at Rachael's, which had begun informally in a living room, and progressed quickly under the direction of Mary Ann Luby, a no-nonsense Dominican nun.

"Before Mary Ann, it was chaotic," Sue says. "She put a structure in place, things like no sleeping during the day, or if you have a drug and alcohol problem, you have to go to the NA/AA meeting before lunch. It taught me a lot—I started out kind of mellow. But people come here who have lost everything. We have to get rid of the lice. We have to find them a place to sleep where they won't be hurt. They have a long way to go." At least half, she says, never get there—"although I still don't think of them as the Chronically Homeless, like they're one big blob or something. They may have their crazy, paranoid lawsuits, and their broken-up families, but they're all different. Some of my clients are annoying. Some are charming."

More than a few are gardeners. "Just about all the women here are black, from the rural South," Sue says. "They've grown food since they were children. When I asked them, they told me to grow them some particular picklin' cukes. Some okra. Lettuce, tomatoes, and peppers."

Last year, the garden's first, Sue planted all that and cutting flowers in between. "I try to keep it dignified and calming," she says. "No red flowers, for instance, but blue and white, and cream-colored nasturtiums."

Mrs. Backhouse bulbs from the original Shankle garden were added last fall. Shepherd's Seeds donated a selection of tomatoes and peppers. Sue added daylilies and globe amaranth, impatiens and moon vine.

"It's kind of how gardening was when I grew up," she decides. "You have little or no money and you have to grow everything. A lot in North Carolina still do it that way, and it's how I do it, too."

Mabel, a thirty-year-old developmentally disabled client, has been helping her—gathering up the sticks that blew down from the trees over the winter, watering, and weeding. "She's my best gardener," Sue says. "She always lived with some drunk old relatives, and when they died, she landed in the shelter, where she was just about eaten alive. I think some teacher must have told her she's slow and stupid."

Not in the garden, where she spends most of the day.

"And I have two others that are faithful about helping me," Sue adds. "They're a lot alike. In their forties. *Very* mentally ill—delusional, really. They both think the government owes them a lot of money. But the garden's outside all of that and we can just work there together. One's a white woman from Florida, obviously very well-bred. She'd never talk to you. The other is Willa. She's a black woman, from Savannah, Georgia. She might."

It takes several months. Finally, with the summer harvest going full bore, I talk to Willa on the phone. "I've been keeping a garden all my life," she says, in a careful, cultured voice. "I have always liked to smell the soil, to watch plants grow, to have my bare feet wet on the sidewalk. No matter what anyone says, it's not a dirty job."

Willa says she has pined for a garden to tend ever since coming to the city to "get with the government about some issues that was plaguing me." Her two children no longer live with her—they have been "dissipated," she says, a little sadly. So her refuge has come to be the Rachael's garden, where she waters and weeds and watches the flowers come into bloom.

"When winter comes, I don't know what I'll do," she admits. "I'd feel a whole lot better if I had a plant. The one I want looks sort of like a snake plant, but with a red flower that comes out around Christmas time."

Her subsidized apartment may or may not have enough light for such a plant. She may or may not still be living there. She may be back in the shelter. She may have won a big money award from suing the government, she points out.

"But I will need something physical," she says. "I will need the garden to take my mind away from what plagues it. I'm forty-four, and this is what I know. Gardening is all there is, while you're doing it."

⚘

The next day, I visit Renee Stephenson Mitchell, whom I have been told is a voracious urban gardener. A thirty-six-year-old public defender, she lives in a posh condominium complex near Georgetown, but answers the door wearing her most comfortable gardening clothes—old jeans, well-worn workboots, a T-shirt with a map of the London Underground on it, and a head scarf. She is tall, thin, strong, and mad.

She tells me her upstairs neighbors, two college girls, kept her up all night with loud music. When Renee called to complain, they asked her, in a dismissive way, who her landlord was. They assumed she rents, she says, because she is black. "I'm the landlord," she tells me, "though I suppose that's hard for them to believe."

Perhaps, I venture, it's because she looks much younger than her thirty-six years.

Perhaps not, Renee Stephenson Mitchell fires back. Denver has not prepared me for matters like these, she says. But that's enough of that. She switches gears and begins talking about British garden writer Vita Sackville-West, whose books are piled up next to her bed.

"Her style is not exactly what I like," Renee says, "but I admire it. I love perennials mixed with a little wild space. An espaliered fruit tree. All that works in an urban garden."

Renee's condo is crammed with stacks of books—half gardening, half law, with a few novels thrown in—and case files leaning in precarious piles. Flowers hang to dry over open cabinet doors. She roots through all this for her gloves—which she never gets around to wearing—and a trowel. We're getting ready to drive to Hannah House, a residence for battered and displaced women, a lot of them devastated, one way or another, by crack.

Renee is starting a garden there. Most of her weekends are taken up with the initial dirt work. I get the impression her social life comes in waves; that I have caught her during an introspective soil-tilling spell. She's been gardening her parents' one-acre suburban yard for ten years now, but this spring she decided she needed something more urban and communal.

First, she investigated the community garden in her neighborhood, but rejected it because "it's so snooty. They told me, we can't have women growing their zucchini vines all over the place," she says. "They said they're tough on neatness. And they have a one-year waiting list for a garden plot."

This was not Renee's style at all—despite the fact that she first learned gardening during summers spent with her grandfather in Guyana. "It was a very British garden," she recalls. "He was heavy into lawn rollers. There was a knot garden for herbs. Formal."

Like anyone who's gardened for twenty years, Renee has developed an individual, almost quirky gardening style. She did not want a bunch of suburban taste mavens telling her to tie back her zucchini vines. Hannah House, located just one block from the inner-city law office her father started in the fifties, was much more appealing. When Renee walked over to survey its fifteen-by-fifteen-foot yard, she found a bare, almost blasted plot of earth dotted with rubble, spent hypodermic needles, and empty crack vials. She liked it. The idea of working with the Hannah House women to build a garden from the ground up appealed to her.

"It would be helping people, I thought," she says, "and I have weird thoughts about helping people. I'm pretty confrontive. I tell people, 'Look, I grew up in the ghetto, too, and I don't have to steal radios to make a living.'" But if that kind of straight talk made the Hannah House women nervous, she thought, they could just garden together. "I know gardening takes the edge off," she says. "And with these women, there's definitely an edge."

Hannah House is another old brownstone in a marginal neighborhood, with weeds growing through a flagstone sidewalk, upon which a priest is talking earnestly to a group of well-dressed white women. "They're trying to buy the building next door," Renee explains. "I guess it would make the program twice as big." She walks right up to the priest and shakes his hand.

"I'm Renee Mitchell, I'm an attorney, I'm working on the Hannah House garden," she says forcefully. There will be no mistaking her for a client.

Inside, four women are sitting quietly in the living room, watching television. In the kitchen, another woman is working on her resumé.

"She helped me weed last week," Renee says, as we walk a narrow path out to the garden. Another resident of the house walks past us on her way back from dumping the garbage in the alley.

"What I'm doing here," Renee says, "is turning over the earth a little, getting rid of some weeds." She hands me a shovel. There are six raised beds, many with volunteer marigold seedlings coming up, some spring bulbs, a clematis getting ready to bloom, and young tomato plants in cages. Several hundred seedlings sit around in flats waiting for a light rain—Renee's favorite transplanting weather.

"I planned all kinds of flowers for back here," she says, "but I realized that what these women really wanted was vegetables. So it's going to be all simple stuff, morning glories along the fence, moonflower, peppers, and tomatoes—Big Boys and Beefsteak. Some okra, maybe some beans."

It sounds workable to me. I stick the spade into the hard, pebble-ridden, almost yellow soil, and begin to double-dig. Beside me, Renee does the same. I don't usually take to gardening with another person, but we work the same way—our pace, our depth of dig, everything.

"You need some compost in here," I say.

"Yeah," she sighs, "but we can't do food scraps around here. Too many rats. They'd eat everything in the garden."

As we work, two women who live at Hannah House are watching us—shy to the point of pain. Something about the way they hold themselves reminds me of prizefighters retired from the ring. Renee talks to them quietly about work—which she has, in abundance—and children, which she does not. She mentions she could use some help weeding. It's hard to tell if they'll commit or not.

"But either way," Renee tells them as they head back into the house, "I'm gonna *be* here."

Though it is only April, it's hot. Both of us are sweating freely. I uncover several flat, desiccated squares of fur that turn out to be dead rats. When it's time for a break, we sit right down in the dirt—another thing we seem to have in common—and start talking about peppers.

"What I want here are the exotic Zapotecs," Renee says. "In Guyana, we use them to make pepper sauce. You grind it in the food processor and then put it in curry and rice. It's so hot you gotta be almost careful.

"I like to cook, but not as a chore," Renee continues. "I don't like to make a nice little dinner every night, but a feast. Oh, I love to grill some smoked flounder rubbed with garlic and olive oil in the summer. And then bake some bread, make pasta, more pesto than I can ever use, with basil out of the garden. Or take skin off the chicken, let it smoke and get all crispy."

We are on our knees in the earth, talking recipes, when two white women in their forties pass by.

"They have these little gardens," one of them is saying, "and it's the cutest thing. The gals get so excited about the fresh tomatoes."

"Are you the gardener?" the other woman asks Renee.

"Actually, I'm an attorney," Renee answers.

"Oh, are you with the Southern Poverty Law Center?"

"No," Renee answers, "I have my own practice."

"Well, that's wonderful. It's nice of *you* to be working here, too," the first woman tells me. "Are you earning a little college money?"

"No," I say. "I'm not in college. I'm thirty-six years old."

On that note, we leave Hannah House for the day—but not before Renee tells several more women, "Remember, I'm gonna *be* here." We stop at Renee's office on the way to her parents' garden. It's a huge old house, weirdly remodeled in the forties, exuding neglect. Renee's father ran a thriving law practice here during the sixties and seventies before being appointed a federal judge.

"I spent a lot of time here when I was a kid," she says. "And it was hard, in a way, coming to work in the ghetto. My parents had become middle class. We had moved to the ivory tower. I went to Sidwell Friends, where Chelsea Clinton goes now. I remember saying, 'I don't want to go to the office with Pops, I want to go to Martha's Vineyard with my friends.' But my Mom would say, 'No, you're going to answer the phone for your father.'"

This began when Renee was nine and she appears to have accepted her fate—becoming everything her father was and more. From Sidwell, she went on to Tufts University and then law school at Georgetown. Like her father's, Renee's practice centers on the black community— "Although," she says, "I have some interesting contacts most black attorneys don't. Anyway," she sighs, "this kind of work takes total patience and acceptance of defeat on a daily basis. I'm surrounded by fetal alcohol syndrome, crack babies, people who just won't work. I'm constantly telling people, 'Look, you don't need two-hundred-dollar sneakers. Just get a job.'"

Once inside her office—where she is currently the only tenant—she debates whether or not to lock the front door. "It's quite a neighborhood," she says. "I don't want anyone coming in the front door, but if they got in some other way, I wouldn't want to be trapped in here with them, either."

Her parents' suburban home, forty-five minutes away in the Colonial Village neighborhood, is another world entirely. "Now please," Renee says, "every gardener will tell you this isn't the right time to see the garden, that it'll look better next month. I'm going to tell you the same thing. I mean, I've only been working this garden for ten years or so. It's all still trowel and error."

In fact, the garden is big, wild, and experimental, with much more attention given to adventure than detail. We eat lunch by an almost decrepit swimming pool surrounded by giant beds of yellow coneflower. Purple loosestrife ranges through a meadow below us, along with red tulips with sensuous black-and-yellow eyes, hundred-year-old white peonies, and clouds of alyssum and campanula. Big sections of earth are turned up everywhere, shovels sticking out. Renee's experiments include a collection of mosses, a bed of sedums, and painstakingly pruned Japanese specimen trees. It is a big place, but private.

"People don't understand what I do in here, by myself, at all," Renee laughs. "If they did, they'd stop giving me gloves, because I can't wear them. I've got to feel the earth in my hands."

For the rest of the weekend, that's what she does.

❦ ☀ ❦

Twenty-four hours later, I arrive in New York City. The air is full of subway exhaust and the smell of rotting garbage. Just the way I remember it, only this is the Bowery, not the Upper West Side. I am standing outside the wrought iron gates of the Liz Christy Bowery Garden, waiting for an outing with the Green Guerrillas.

"It's my parish, babe," said Phil "the Gardener" Tietz, one of two acting heads of the guerrillas. "We'll have an old-style Green Guerrillas day."

Tietz has been a guerrilla for more than ten years, but he has no idea how the organization came to be, except that its emergence coincided with the beginning of the Liz Christy garden at Third and Houston. Liz Christy, a gardening visionary who died in 1985, at forty, of cancer, started with a hippy-era community vegetable plot and turned it, with the help of neighbors, into a rarified landscape. While she was tilling the soil, the Green Guerrillas were running wild at night, delivering compost, seeds, and plants to community gardens all over the Lower East Side. In the beginning, they were thoroughly anonymous—a handful of militants who, if they saw a vacant lot they liked, simply moved in and began gardening, without asking anyone's permission.

Today there are more than forty gardens in the Lower East Side, some officially sanctioned, others run by gardeners the guerrillas think of as squatters. The Green Guerrillas are still distributing advice and plant material, but in a much more official, funded way. You can usually find at least a few guerrillas at the Christy garden, now surrounded by a high cast-iron fence with garbage blown against it, and sometimes small white paper voodoo packages tied to it with black thread. "I don't open them," Phil says. "I'm putting enough of a hex on myself by touching them. I think there are feathers inside." The Liz Christy gardeners work on everything from perennial borders to beehives to artificial ponds to fruit trees.

Looking through the fence, I can see the fifty trash sacks full of dead leaves Phil plans to distribute today—as well as however much horse manure he can cajole out of Manhattan's eleven livery stables. For transportation, his partner, Patricia Jasaitis, who is on loan from the city compost program, has rented a van so ancient it appears to be held together with wire and duct tape.

"So," she says, after introducing herself, "shall we move some leaves? They're going anaerobic." She can tell by their rotten, acrid smell.

But instead of hauling leaves, Patricia and I step over a few sleeping winos and into the Liz Christy garden, where she takes me on a very relaxed tour.

Patricia is a tall, heroically proportioned woman with a long blond braid down her back. She wears heavy-duty hiking boots, baggy shorts, and a black turtleneck. She looks like a granola girl of my vintage— Bryn Mawr College class of 1980, if I had not dropped out—but she is only twenty-three. She attended a private girls' school in Manhattan, worked summer jobs at botanical gardens, majored in botany, and finally let her interest in urban gardens lead her back to New York.

She is a New York girl who deliberately dresses and acts as rural as possible. This is handy when it comes time to use the Liz Christy bathroom—a two-quart Tupperware jug located in a shed. When it is my turn to use it, I have an oddly Adirondack sensation, despite the sounds of wheezing bus doors and screaming delivery men.

When I emerge, I find Phil the Gardener waiting impatiently for us by the holding area. He is a short, stocky man in low-slung jeans, an old T-shirt, and tattered gardening gloves. But his posture is at all times erect and graceful.

"Yeah, so I came here to become a dancer," Phil explains, in his adopted Brooklynese accent. "As it turns out, I became a gardener who slings shit. In 1978, there was a garbage strike on my block. These people at the stable on Forty-fifth Street couldn't get their manure carted away. It lasted two weeks, with the horseshit piling up, and I decided to start a block garden. Eventually we spread it all out and it became our front lawn."

On his off-hours from the guerrillas, Phil works in three different community gardens for pleasure. He is never without a gardening obsession. In recent years, it has taken the form of a frantic desire to "knock off Smith and Hawken. I even teach a class in how to make that expensive shit by yourself at home. It's very popular," he says, grinning widely.

Today is the dawn of a new Phil passion. Hops.

"It's the thing with me," he confirms. Having loaded up the leaves, we are driving through an obstacle course of delivery trucks to a local brew pub. "You know what? I think I'm gonna visit the New York City Homebrewers Guild and tell them hops used to be a big thing in the Hudson Valley," Phil says. "They *can* be grown here. That's what I'm gonna tell these dudes. I mean, why ship this shit from England?"

At Captain Nick's R&R Bar, the manager is polite but perplexed, but then he does not speak enough English to grasp Phil's latest concept—that hops ought to be sown on tenement roof tops and trained to grow down strings until they reach the street. "At the end of the growing season, you just cut the strings and down they fall," Phil explains.

Patricia cuts in. What she would like, she explains patiently, is the spent hops left over from the brewing process. It will make great compost, she says. The manager does not seem to understand the request. She will have to come back a few more times, she decides.

So will Phil—but his assignment will be to drink and carouse. "Hey, one time I hung with a bunch of Latvian guys here. They taught me some Latvian drinking songs, and after awhile," he says proudly, "people complained."

On our way south, near the Battery, we stop at a brand-new garden on the grounds of a private school. The newly dug beds are sandwiched between two very busy sidewalks. The requisite crack vials have already landed in the furrows. We leave three bags of leaves and one of manure. When I touch the soil, it is too hard to crumble—and this after a medium rain last night. I can't imagine how any crop, even a weed, could grow here, let alone how anyone could pulverize it with a shovel.

"It's the perfect blend of Manhattan soil," Phil tells me. "Just enough soil, just enough clay, and just enough sand to form cement. You ain't seen nothin' yet! That's not even big city rubble!"

That comes next, in a classic squatter garden dug into a space between two tenements, where a demolition crew knocked an old brick building into its own cellar. Fifteen feet beneath this layer is the solid granite backbone of Manhattan—and sometimes an aquifer. "You can tell, if a willow tree starts to grow out of it," Phil says. Anyone who gardens here has not only had to bring in topsoil by the wheelbarrow load, but has probably spent weeks smoking out rats' nests and picking up old hypodermics. Each individual plot is jealously protected by chainlink and chickenwire fencing, giving it the look of a garden in a war zone, which, in some ways, it is. Phil points out homemade solar collectors and a windmill on top of the building next door. "Anarchists occupy that place, for sure," he says.

"How can you tell?" I ask.

"See all the tarps where the windows should be? We call that Tompkins Square blue. That's how you tell," he says. In this neighborhood, anarchist squatters are part of the landscape. Therefore, Phil loves them—is, in fact, fascinated by them.

"Not only that," he shouts suddenly, as we approach the El Sol Community Garden, "there's a BVM! Blessed Virgin Mary, to you," he tells me. "Hey! There's two! We should give them a goodly amount of shit."

He climbs into the back of the van, unloads two burlap sacks full of horse manure, and flings them over the garden fence. It is no mean feat, the fence being ten feet tall. Inside it, the BVMs sparkle from inside homemade bathtub shrines. Roses are growing inside cages. The garden paths are narrow, the corn is already knee-high, the bulbs blazing in a very un–Martha Stewart way. The people who garden here have left their possessions lying around—hoes, rakes, shovels, children's playground toys. I have read those stories in *Sunset* magazine about creating the "outdoor living room," but this is the real thing—it looks as if a whole family has left, but only briefly, perhaps to go out for pizza. When they get back, they will, no doubt, be surprised and heartened at the sight of the two sacks of horse manure that have appeared mysteriously.

"Hell's Kitchen," Phil murmurs, as we drive north. "It's going to be so peaceful here in summer, when all the white people are gone."

It doesn't seem to signify that Phil the Gardener could not be much whiter himself. Born and bred in Kansas, he now considers himself at home in the polyglot slums of lower Manhattan. And maybe, if there's time, Harlem.

The next three gardens are classic examples of the gift-shop-on-acid style Patricia calls the *chotchke-shmatte* garden—vegetables, cherry trees, flowers, and folk-art sculpture all mixed together. A thirty-foot-tall pole supports a plaster horse with vines growing up it; a carved sheet metal fence shoots up next to baby sunflowers.

"I don't know about all that," says Patricia, who is on the board of her local community garden and is currently involved in a dispute between *shmatte* lovers and those who prefer classic, simple garden lines. "I used to like the *chotchke-shmatte* thing myself," she says. "Now I'm a little sick of it."

But enough idle chatter. We are dangerously low on horseshit. In front of a midtown hansom cab stable, Patricia and Phil pull on their gloves. Having gardened gloveless all my life, I hesitate—but only until I grasp the nature of our job. Inside the stable, we prepare to shovel a mixture of manure-and-urine-soaked straw and shavings into half-rotted burlap coffee sacks. Because the stable has three stories, this mixture has to be dumped through holes in the ceiling, in a laundry-chutelike manner. On the first floor, it all empties into a commodious dumpster, where we stand, bags and pitchforks in hand, waiting for it to fill up—until a hostler with an intimidating Irish brogue tells us to be quick about it, as we're blocking the equine traffic.

Showing off, I offer to jump into the dumpster and shovel from there. No one tries to stop me. Within seconds, I am sunk up to my knees in the wettest, most pungent dung I have ever known, and being an avid composter, I have known some. We gather up a good thirty sacks and are just preparing to leave, when the ceiling vent opens up and sprays me with a light but thorough coat of manure from head to toe.

"Hey," Phil says, after a short silence, "did you know Sir Thomas Lipton invented the tea bag because of horse manure? His gardeners were steeping burlap bags of horseshit in water to make manure tea. It gave Sir Thomas the idea."

For the rest of the day, we deliver horse manure to pockets of dirt all over lower Manhattan. The gardeners we meet are long-suffering, full of joy nonetheless, bilingual, trilingual, and Spanish-speaking-only. Blessed virgins and blessed pagans roost side by side. As usual, crazy people seem called to work the soil. As usual, there are sloppy gardens and crops planted in straight lines; community organizational boards and anarchy in action. Every single one of them is thrilled at the prospect of free horse manure.

It's a powerful substance. At the end of the day, I begin to walk toward the West Village, where I have planned to attend a ballet class. It quickly becomes clear, however, that I am smellier than any roomful of sweating ballerinas could hope to be. On the train to Long Island, during rush hour, I have a whole bank of seats to myself. That night, after a half-hour-long shower, I determine that my shoes and watch are so penetrated with horse pee as to be worthless, and I throw them away.

But I'm too happy to care. I have learned that even in what is arguably the most urban city in the world, you can farm openly, happily, almost midwesternly. You can grow your own food, you can make soil out of broken bricks, you can even throw a barbecue in your garden, stand around drinking beer and listening to the crickets thrum. I know, because that's what Phil and the Liz Christy gardeners do—on the first Tuesday of every month, and any time there's a full moon. "You should come," Phil has said. "The moon should be full in about a week."

5 Estates

Did you ever think how a bit of land shows the character of the owner?

LAURA INGALLS WILDER

According to my father, the Chotzinoff family
motto is *More Is Better*. My father is usually flat broke, but he still
believes earthly things should be expensive and rare. Throughout his
life, his relatives, spouses, and loved ones have found this attitude
alarming. My father doesn't care.

"I didn't learn this from a bunch of peasant ancestors," he points out.
"I made it up myself."

My dad's definition of the More-Is-Better landscape is very specific:
understated, huge, and green. Manicured privet and rolling lawns. An
estate. "You know," he says, "taste. It's how rich people's houses look on
the outside, just like on the inside they all have that chintz and those
porcelain statues of dogs. You know."

I do know. He's thinking of when he first met my mother, and the
gentleman's farm in Holmdel, New Jersey, where she grew up.

As a child, I was taken there on weekends and always for Thanksgiving. Holmdel had that look—porcelain dogs and flowered chintz, but
also cracked leather armchairs and faded photographs of people on
horses. I remember Holmdel mostly in the heat of June: the rows of
windbreak trees, the soybean fields, the sweet smell of horse manure
and big boxwood hedges that smelled like wet dogs. The bees that
careened through open windows into the house were enormous, fuzzy,
and loud.

My mother says she never grew attached to Holmdel because there
were no blacktop roads on the farm, and therefore no place to roller
skate. But my sister, my cousins, and I loved it. We spent our time there
finding shark's teeth in an ancient stream bed, eating and playing and
living outside in a world that could not have been more different than
Manhattan. My sister, now a top-flight horse trainer, learned to ride in
Holmdel. It was also in Holmdel, while visiting my favorite great aunt
at the farm next door, that I heard her introduce her gardener as "my
little earth man who grows the vegetables."

Pete, the gardener in question, not only didn't mind being referred to as Aunt Laura's little earth man, but was mildly flattered by it. He was shy and, I think, it made him feel interesting. Occasionally, when I was full of adolescent angst, this seemed wrong: How could I love a place that only looked the way it did because it was maintained by a corps of little earth men? But then, because I'm my father's daughter, I would think, *Well, it's owned by a relative.*

❧ ✸ ☙

It is fall in western Louisiana. I am in the middle of a five-thousand-mile road trip. While gazing idly at my road atlas, I notice the existence of something called Live Oak Gardens. On the telephone, I speak to a gardener named Bryan Riche, who tells me Live Oak is a restored plantation home, as well as a twenty-acre tourist attraction. Good, I think. A genuine Southern estate.

I drive to New Iberia on a cold, nasty day. The sky is black with rain, and even when it stops, the land I pass through has an ominous, almost gothic look. Trucks loaded precariously with sugarcane slam past. I turn off on a one-mile-long driveway lined with live oaks. Weird trees—their exposed roots look like huge, bony fingers. Suddenly, a house pops out of the horizon—a big white cake of a house. It looms on a hill overlooking the intercoastal waterway.

Unless you count me, there are no tourists. Bryan Riche won't be here for another two hours, but he has kindly invited me to drive around the grounds in a golf cart, which I do, on gravel paths, in the whipping wind, past beds and beds of tended roses, lilies, annual flowers, shrubs. From up on the hill the white house glares at me. I ride very fast past its dining-room windows, causing them to shake. The rooms I can see are cordoned off with velvet ropes. Then I joyride down to the dock over the Gulf of Mexico, where a launch is moored. A disembodied chimney rises out of the water, surrounded by the charred stumps of lightning-struck trees. I look at this view for a long time, contemplating Jean Lafitte, the pirate who once plied these waters, and enjoying the swish of Spanish moss in the trees.

But I don't love these gardens. They are sterile—like the plantings in southern California mall parking lots, where holes in the concrete are neatly stuffed with flowering plants. (Never a weed, never a dying leaf.) At Live Oak Gardens, I see rows of annuals, a water garden, a huge collection of daylilies.

Then I see Bryan Riche walking toward me in a suede jacket, jeans, and knee-high rubber boots. He is freezing.

"Time to go home and eat you some *soup*, babe," he says, by way of a greeting, in a voice anyone would peg as Cajun. (Same with the term "babe," which implies nothing flirtatious in this part of the world.) As we huddle around the space heater in his small office, Riche says he is twenty-eight, recently divorced, and has been a gardener all his life.

"My grandmother had a garden and she never *could* get anything to grow," he recalls. "Either the water was so high or the pH was wrong. But yet, I liked working there. In fact, I loved it. I would practically stay there all summer."

His father was more successful—he grew soybeans, cotton, and grain for a dairy and was, for a time, "the director of mosquito control for the whole county." Bryan says this with pride.

I note that just about all the gardeners I've met, in western Louisiana and everywhere else, are virulently opposed to spraying for mosquitoes. "I don't know why," Bryan says stoutly. "I tell you, mosquitoes around here, they *bad*. We have to spray like crazy at Live Oak. How else you gon' grow camellias, azaleas, or gardenias? I mean, this is twenty acres of intensely managed land. There's really no way organics could keep it all up. But even pests and disease aren't the worst of it. Last year," he sighs, "we lost sixty-five of the live oaks to Hurricane Andrew. Some of our gardens just ain't no more. Hey, babe, when the north wind blows and the water comes up, you can catch minnows in the cisterns."

Small disasters happen weekly around here—drowned flowers, live oaks "fixing to split." But the last big debacle happened in 1980, when Bryan was in high school.

"Back then," he says, "all that water you see was a rich man's backyard. There was a salt dome out there and Texaco went out to drill in it, and they created a kind of whirlpool. It sucked down the salt and oil and sixty acres of gardens. That chimney you see out there belonged to a British guy who lived here just so he could grow his camellias. They all went down inside that dome."

Bryan turns away from this destructive scene. He would rather talk of Japanese landscapes, or promote his upcoming exhibit of historic nosegays. I wait, and the subject changes to Louisiana sugarcane.

"Oh, we all worked in the cane at one time or another, babe," Bryan says. "But back in the slave days, the cane was good to the blacks. They would live in tent houses, they had fireplaces and a place to cook, they never had to worry about health insurance or job security."

"They didn't get paid, either," I point out.

"Yeah," Bryan says, "but I wonder if it wasn't better for them."

⚜

The next spring, while in Washington, D.C., I decide to take in Historic Virginia Garden Week. Virginia is crawling with plantation gardens, I hear, some of them run by the very people who live in the grand old houses on the grounds. I hope to find a fabulously wealthy Virginia Garden Lady.

Along the James River, where land holdings are vast, some of them dating back to the 1600s, I make an arbitrary stop at a place called Brandon Plantation. There, a woman in handkerchief linen and a straw hat takes my ten dollars and directs me down a tree-lined driveway. In front of the house, I see a black jockey statue and what seem like miles of boxwood and moss-covered brick. The smell of the box is heavenly hot. Here and there about the grounds are Yankee tourists dressed in running shorts, black socks, and sandals. There are forty acres to see.

Two hours have elapsed by the time I have walked every meandering path, looked inside every opening in the box, surveyed every one of the perennial borders from every angle. At the end of the widest green path is a huge stone urn and a slight cliff leading down to the James River. Everything is so grand and massive that I begin to feel a bit grand and massive myself, and the tourists attempting refined southern accents and making cracks about the Old South begin to annoy me. I duck through a hedge into a hidden garden. There are four kinds of forsythia, a brick-lined shallow pool, and several cherub statues striking attitudes. I sit on an ancient wire bench, remembering a Howard Nemerov poem I studied in high school:

> Alone at the end of green allées, alone
> Where a path turns back on itself, or else
> Where several paths converge, green bronze, grey stone,
> The weatherbeaten famous figures wait
> Inside their basins, on their pedestals,
> Till time, as promised them, wears out of date . . .

A garden worker in a blue uniform scuttles through the hedge, almost on her knees, and begins to cut back the pachysandra.

94

"Who owns all this?" I ask her.

"Miz Daniel," she replies.

"Is it fun working in a garden like this?"

"Ma'am?" I notice the sweat running into her eyes. It's not *her* garden, I realize. Also, she looks about sixteen. I remember the "fun" of weeding someone else's garden when I was sixteen.

"Do you think I could talk to Miz Daniel?" I ask.

"Oh no. She's *busy.*"

I walk up to the Brandon house anyway. It is red brick with wings, and the kind of beautiful symmetry that, in these parts, usually means Thomas Jefferson had something to do with it. Sure enough, on an official tour guided by more Virginia Garden Ladies in linen, I learn that though the oldest part of the house dates to 1619, its main wing was designed by Jefferson. In the ornate drawing room, our guide directs us to "one of the only pictures ever painted of Robert E. Lee out of uniform." There is a clock that once belonged to Marie Antoinette. Velvet ropes keep us from getting too close to any of it—but the Daniels, whoever they are, actually live here. Presumably their guests socialize on this furniture. Not that the atmosphere is stuffy. (I don't believe Thomas Jefferson ever did stuffy.) The plaster around the front door still shows the four-inch gouges of cannonballs from the Civil War. I ask our guide what the odds are of having a word with Miz Daniel.

"Oh, I don't think so," she replies, "Miz Daniel is very, very busy."

From the hallway comes a throaty, husky, but ever-so Virginian voice. "*Who's* too busy?" it says.

Miz Daniel appearing on her own porch could not have done it better if she were directed by David O. Selznick. A lithe, ageless woman of medium height, she is dressed in a schoolgirlish navy blue skirt and white linen shirt, with a perfectly plain, perfectly beautiful straw hat on her head—which she removes every so often to wave about as if it were a fan. Her hair and skin are both a sort of silvery white.

"So you came to see the garden?" she says. "Why don't we walk down together?"

As we progress down the main allée to the James, she gives me a brief history of her holding. "This garden predates the house, and the house is three hundred years old," she says. "The balance and symmetry are what make it. It's a lot of house."

Miz Daniel has only held sway over Brandon for fifteen years. She is Mister Daniel's second wife and, as such, was expected to take her place in the lineage of his female relatives who have run the place since 1925. The first was Mr. Daniel's mother, who had "help—six in the house and six in the garden." Miz Daniel says her resources were far more limited. So was the future her husband envisioned for her.

"Mister Daniel brought me here and said: I want you to take care of the garden," she says. "So I did. I had worked in a hospital, I had to learn how to support myself, you know. After my divorce I didn't know how to do anything but be a maid."

Miz Daniel looked over the thirty-five acres entrusted to her—"most of it leggy azaleas," she recalls—and began thinking over what she knew of gardens. There had been an orchid collection during her Palm Beach years, but it offered little practical experience. Eventually, she climbed into a pair of overalls and went out to work alongside two black laborers who'd been trained by the federal Green Thumb project.

"One of them was called Mr. Charity," Miz Daniel recalls. Mr. Charity was apparently so unaccustomed to doing manual labor alongside a rich white woman that he practically never said a word. "There was one time," she recalls. "We were digging out a boxwood, and he said: 'Lord, Miz Ann, that's big enough to bury a mule in.' Excuse me."

Miz Daniel interrupts herself because something almost imperceptible has gone wrong. A man who has been hired to drive an enormous lawnmowing tractor has been *collecting the clippings*. "Oh dear," Miz Daniel says. "He hadn't ought to be doing that at all." She runs across the lawn, swinging her hat. Bits of their conversation drift over to me. "Don't get all exhausted now," she tells him. "It's awfully hot."

"Well, it's just very hard to remind them how to do their job," she says, rejoining me on the path. "Some of them don't show up at all, and then they want their job back. About six months ago I hired a man to run the garden for me. I gave him a big salary and a house. He believed in plenty of ten-ten-ten fertilizer and wood chips. Well, he lasted six months. I remember walking through this garden right here and saying to my husband, Robert, what in the *world* has he done with these ornamentals? But Bob laughed it off. He says I just like to tell people what to do."

Luckily, Miz Daniel quickly became an expert. Working "seven to five, with one hour for lunch," she spent the next five years on her grounds, learning the fine art of composting, with occasional afternoons in meetings of her local garden club.

"The garden club women were very concerned about raising money for historical preservation," she recalls. "The Historic Virginia Garden Week started with women driving around with their chauffeurs and having the chauffeurs cut down billboards, you know."

This was marginally interesting, but Miz Daniel soon discovered that her "focus was *not* on growing pretty flowers to put in the house. I consider myself a dirt gardener," she says. "I love to dig. I also love chicken manure."

On a big piece of land like this—and with a big budget—you could have a high old time ordering truckloads of chicken manure, digging enormous holes, and communing with the soil. Right now, Miz Daniel is describing the incredible contortions she's gone through to produce a rose garden.

"We took all the dirt out and put in compost, fertilizer, and gypsum, put the roses back in," she relates. "Still no good roses, so we put in an irrigation system. That didn't work either, so I bought some horse manure, took all the soil and roses out again, *re*dug the beds. And now they're gorgeous." There are close to fifty plants in the bed in question, most of them everblooming hybrid teas.

"Now here's a shrub that smells better if you walk by it fast," she informs me, as we head down the box-lined path to the Necessary House, circa 1765. "Other than that, it really is a treasure, and see these cuts I made on it? Lovely, idn't it? Nobody cuts anything on this place but me, ever, no one. I want a big weeping tree over here. What do you suggest?"

Being totally ignorant of weeping trees, I admire the white iris instead.

"Yes, why not pure colors?" she agrees. "I feel the same thing about daylilies. Why do people grow those tissue paper things?"

Inside the 1928 greenhouse, she surveys a table of perennial seedlings. Water condenses on panes of glass. "Hot enough to make me just *sick*," Miz Daniel observes, fanning with her hat. "And yet I really, really do think this is therapeutic. If you work in the garden, you don't get cancer. And the miracle of that little seed," she says, shaking a packet of lavender. "How God can make something so wonderful out of something so . . . nothing. Would you like some iced tea?"

Miz Daniel fixes it herself. She brings the two glasses to the kitchen table, casually, on a silver tray. The room we sit in is gleaming with the patina of old wood.

"Blacks," she says, without preamble. "It's such a shame they don't like to garden anymore, don't you think? They're good at it, that and taking care of children, but they feel it's beneath them. Sad, idn't it?"

❧ ☀ ☙

It is fall again. In a basement classroom, I read quiz questions over a student's shoulder:

> *Answer briefly with key words indicating that you understand the answers:*
>
> *What is fertility?*
>
> *What is dead?*
>
> *What is alive?*
>
> *Does gardening open any doors for you on the contemplative life?*

When our instructor, landscape designer Bob Howard, has finished handing out the quizzes, he tells us something I already know—that a compost pile should be about as wet as a wrung-out sponge. Then something I'd never thought of: "The idea of a weed is conceptual," he says. "It kind of means *bad guys*. But weeds are very strong characters. To change our attitude about weeds and make them part of our lives should be our goal."

Actually, my goal is still to find an estate garden and an estate gardener I can love, which is why I am attending the Garden World class in the first place. Bob Howard teaches environmental science here at Naropa Institute, in Boulder, Colorado, but he also designs Boulder gardens. Big, expensive ones, I've heard—an interesting career choice for a college professor who has just said this about the moneyed classes:

"Humans get too attached to living in high-rise apartments and watching TV and going down the elevator to the garage and never, never going outside. Humans definitely become too attached to making the money to pay for all that. I will be making that case throughout this course."

What I know about Naropa Institute I learned during the summer of 1976, which I spent here hoping that a dose of eastern thought would make me calm—perhaps even ecstatic. But calm and ecstatic I was not; none of us were at Naropa.

We spent hours absorbing the teachings of Naropa founder and Tibetan mystic Chögyam Trungpa, Rinpoche—who was not just a

98

spiritually advanced man, but a roiling drunk, as anyone who ever attended a party with him can attest. And yet, in the years since my exposure to Trungpa, I have had enough psychotherapy to choke a horse—and none of it has ever worked as well as what he said about staying in the present moment. I can't say the same for anything I learned at Naropa's Jack Kerouac School of Disembodied Poetics—its pretentious name still makes me cringe—but I do love Naropa's favorite saying: *The love of wisdom puts us on the spot all the time.* Hitchhiking back east at the end of the summer of 1976, with nothing but a guitar and a T-shirt to my name, I was on the spot, all right, but could you call it wisdom? By that time, I was not only burned out on the world of "contemplative studies," but on education itself.

I never went back to college, in any form, but here I am at Naropa, again, and nothing seems to have changed. The stringy, ethnic look of the mid-seventies is back with a vengeance among people half my age. During a break, I stand in a field of grass beneath six Tibetan prayer flags and find them beautiful, almost inspirational. But then I wander over to the garden Bob Howard and his students have made, and notice nothing much more than weeds, which are being allowed to flourish unfettered.

And that's the way the rest of the Garden World class goes. I am alternately infuriated by pat political correctness and charmed.

Now Bob Howard discusses his past. Like Beth Benjamin at Shepherd's, he learned to garden from British zealot Alan Chadwick. For a time, he lived and worked at Chadwick's seventeen-acre herb farm in northern California. He was twenty-three at the time. "I was very tied to my verbal nature and had disregarded my body," he recalls. "Gardening almost made me have roots in my boots."

It's hard to completely dismiss anyone with roots in his boots. After class, I come straight to the point. "Find me a rich woman," I say. "Please."

For a beat or two, he gives me that probing Buddhist look. Then he gives me a phone number.

ॐ ☀ ॐ

At Wayne and Janny Goss's house in Boulder, Hank Williams pours from the radio in the kitchen and two black standard poodles cruise through the shrubbery. Blue delphiniums in huge clay bowls are beginning their second bloom. A low hedge of lavender releases a cloud of scent when I kick it accidentally. I am standing on the Gosses' seven-acre spread in the middle of a pretty modest neighborhood that abuts the Boulder foothills. The Goss place is by far the most expensive and luxurious in a two-mile radius. From the street, faced with the bamboo fence that encircles the property, you see almost nothing.

"That's the idea," Janny says. "I don't necessarily want anyone to see anything." Right now, at the center of the compound, Janny is sitting at a wrought-iron table on one of her four slate patios, drinking Very Veggie juice. She is wearing Birkenstock clogs, a flannel shirt, and baggy shorts. She looks to be in her early forties, but I get the feeling her style has barely changed in the past two decades.

Susan Spalding, the almost-full-time gardener who supervises these seven acres, comes from the same sartorial family. She wears baggy denim and flannel, her long gray hair falling over one eye. Susan and Janny have spent more than three years of mornings sitting here, talking about the gardens within the garden. Today, they're designing a thicket.

"We're planning to make it look unplanned," says Susan. "But plans rise and fall apart around here. You see those viburnums with phosphorescent orange berries? Right next to them are phosphorescent pink dianthus. It was a terrible combination."

"We'll redo it," says Janny. "Like these myrtle beds. We changed them this year, made them bigger so the house doesn't feel . . . "

"Squished," offers Susan.

"Yes," Janny agrees. "All the myrtle beds were too little. They made the house look . . . "

"Doilied," Susan decides. "And about these shrubs. The point was, you wanted them to be sentinels—"

"Sentinels? Did I say that?"

"No, I just thought of it, but it's what you meant. Anyway," Susan tells me, "there's a lot of sitting and looking and asking everyone's opinions to get it to look this way."

"A lot of standing around pretending to be a tree," Janny adds, striking a branched pose.

I have been here less than five minutes, but already I covet this place. Anchored by a new house in a hundred-year-old orchard, it has everything: countless little gardens that seem to spring wildly out of the underbrush, treehouses in the gnarled old apple trees, a sweeping but still dandeliony lawn with blue spruces at its edge, and at every point of the compass, anywhere you might want to kill some time *not* garden-ing, a bench or a chair or a grassy place to collapse upon. Besides, it's a democracy. Dogs are not just allowed, but encouraged.

"This garden absorbs dogs," Janny agrees. "It also swallows up kids and croquet and soccer. The first thing I did when we moved here was trees. We had no furniture for years and years. Instead, we kept putting in evergreens. Bob Howard was instrumental. We'd go out into the yard at night, and he'd see a neighbor's light. The next day we'd plant a tree to screen it. Or we'd go upstairs and experience the view *down*. We spent a lot of time looking down from all the upstairs windows. I must have put in fifty evergreens. In my mind, they count as furniture. And then Susan came, and she's really made me aware of textures, leaf patterns, twig against twig."

"Because I had an epiphany about you," Susan says. "What you really want here is the Adirondacks."

That would make sense. Born and raised in the rural area around Cincinnati, Janny spent summers with her family in the Adirondacks and Maine.

"What I remember about Cincinnati were infinite fields, horses, trails, and daffodils," Janny says. "My mother planted thousands of daffodils, scilla, and snowdrops. I felt like I was inside a poster my grandmother painted for the Garden Club of America, where this fairy was sitting inside a flower saying *enjoy, don't destroy*. And in the Adirondacks, those thickets, that wilderness . . . the winters are so harsh there that when you see a flower in the woods, it seems like a miracle."

Married young, Wayne and Janny moved to Boulder in 1970. Wayne went to the University of Colorado for a business degree. Janny raised two children and studied pottery until she was good enough at it to hold small sales on the front porch of the hundred-year-old miner's shack where they lived. Bob Howard turned out to be a neighbor. The first suggestion he made was that the ancient privet hedge that surrounded the property could use some trimming. Other projects followed: a stone wall, a sodded lawn, spring bulbs. Janny discovered that, although she'd been more accustomed to frolicking in gardens than working in them, she found deep satisfaction in "choosing one little spot to work on, choosing a new one every year."

The miner's shack garden evolved one spot at a time for sixteen years. "It was awful to leave," Janny recalls. "I can't go back and look at it now."

But it was time to move, and this was a move up. Seven acres in the middle of Boulder—a city where the price of everything is inflated—did not come cheap. But by 1986, Wayne was doing well as a venture capitalist. For their money, the Gosses got a fire-blighted orchard and a run-down house.

"We didn't mean to take it all down," Janny says, "but we wanted to feel the sun passing through the house." All the windows their architect designed required a landscape. Janny hired Bob Howard to dream up the kind you could "look out at, and be pleased."

Now eight years old, it is maintained not just by Janny—who weeds and prunes for hours each day during the growing season—but by a lawn crew, a "sprinkler genius," rototillers, stone fitters, tree experts, and general laborers.

Susan Spalding, who took over from Bob Howard as the designated landscape designer, comes by almost daily. "But I'm not in *charge* of any of the people," Susan says. "It's a different kind of garden that way. It's more like I putter. I spend as much time talking with Janny as I do digging. But I'm always paid. With Janny, it's time and materials. She has a personal relationship with everyone who works on this land. I like it that way. Things never get too hoity-toity."

I watch as Janny and Susan lay out the edge of a perennial border with a hose. They have decided to make it three feet wider. Neither is in a hurry about it. The hose is moved, nudged over a half foot, recurved. Hours, or even days, will go by before anyone starts digging.

"This border is still in transition," Janny says. "Realize that. It took how many hours of discussion this spring?"

"Lots," Susan says.

"But that's not all we talk about when we're working together," Janny says. "We talk about life, or beauty, or surprises."

"Or *oh, look, remember when we planted that?*"

"I have this tool, a kind of three-pronged hoe, a kind of comb," Janny says. "I love to have the soil kind of loose. I like to scratch it, churn it up. And I will do that sometimes and not talk at all and think of nothing."

"You know," Susan observes, "this whole year has been that way. It's as if we *all* relaxed."

"We did," Janny agrees. Then she drops the hose and falls silent for a moment. "There's something else," she says. "My younger brother died of AIDS this spring. I was so taken with the garden he and his lover had made. After he died, we all gathered there, in Maine, and we put his ashes on a raft with firecrackers and white peonies and lilacs, and we watched it go out onto the pond. We sat and talked about him, and none of the children were cranky and no one was stung by a wasp."

As she talks, Janny wanders north to a small vegetable garden surrounded by an overgrown grapevine. "When I came back home, I thought: I want to become a *part* of this land," she continues. "And I knew it would take more money, but I thought, let's just do it. We may not any of us have years left."

"So it's been a different year," Susan confirms. "We did a lot, but we were relaxed."

I thump down into a wooden chair, lifting my face up to the dappled light and admiring an overgrown grapevine.

"Yes, because it looks like an old sway-backed horse," says Janny. "You're supposed to prune it, but I don't. I like the muscle of it, and the way the twigs look in winter. I like to sit in that chair, too," she adds. "I like to sit there and look toward home."

❧ Blue Border ❧

A vista of flowers, seen from twenty feet away while seated in a comfortable chair, ought to be mostly big and mostly blue—at least I think so. Janny Goss, Susan Spalding, and Bob Howard have taken this idea and made it better with splashes of white, yellow, and even chartreuse. Here's what they planted in my favorite of the Goss borders:

Aster alpinus

Campanula carpatica Blue Chips

Delphinium (Blue Bird and Black Knight)

Heuchera

Iris pseudacorus

Lady's mantle

Monarda

Nicotiana (any white)

Peony (any white)

Salvia Victoria

Syringa japonica

6 Long Island Roots

Daffodil time is past.
This is summer, summer!

WILLIAM CARLOS WILLIAMS, "THE IVY CROWN"

"Now here," says my aunt Cookie Grossman, "is a truly rustic hat." The hat is what remains of a straw planter saved from a wire-service flower arrangement. Aunt Cookie puts it on. It has a big hole on the crown, through which her hair pokes. She is also wearing the kind of baggy white canvas pants you see on sailors in pirate movies, Uncle Herb's long-sleeved shirt, and old, worn Keds.

Twenty years ago, when I first began hanging around this garden, there was one vegetable bed, about eight feet long and three feet wide. I remember sitting on the outside stairs watching Aunt Cookie plant a bag of white onion sets, and then write in her garden journal for June: *Planted bag of white onion sets.* It was a moment as specific as the day I learned to read. I recall watching Aunt Cookie garden for another hour or so and thinking *I am, for some reason I don't understand at all, very interested in this.* I was sixteen.

There are no onion sets in that original bed anymore. There are at least twenty more beds now, and this one is crowded with tall blue flowers. Platycodon, Aunt Cookie says. Although she had nothing to do with it.

"Everything moves around on its own in this garden, if you've noticed," she says. "It used to be yellow and orange flowers right here. Now the whole thing is blue." Aunt Cookie's garden has become a sort of reseeding mecca. The plants settle where they feel like it. Since my last visit, I notice that the coreopsis has moved several arcs in a clockwise direction, while the dill is spread indiscriminately from compost pile to rosebush. White alyssum pours from the holes in what used to be an ugly cinderblock retaining wall. Aunt Cookie's garden, generally accepted to be the flagship of this hundred-house boardwalk beach community, has become a jungle. You used to be able to see her house from the sidewalk. Now, all you see is green, and maybe a glimpse of that truly rustic hat.

On the last day of July, it is damply hot here, with an incessant cicada hiss in the background. Mosquitoes hover and whine around our ankles. A piano tuner's intermittent plunking floats from a second-story window. It's a languorous tuning job—Uncle Herb and the tuner once played in the same symphony, and they are catching up between tones. I feel content and slightly sleepy, as if I had lived this same day, with this same weather, and these same piano notes, since I was a child.

In every room of Aunt Cookie and Uncle Herb's house are stacks of books, paintings I have stared at since childhood, furniture I slept on, played on, and did what I could to destroy. The ghosts of my dead relatives—all of them musicians, all of them probably still quipping in the grave—are in every thread of every rug, on every shelf within every dish, on the deck in canvas lounge chairs, drinking vodka and eating clams on a summer evening. Even among the living, not much has changed. I could be nine, or nineteen, or twenty-nine—just one of the of relatives.

But out in the yard, with Aunt Cookie, I am thirty-six, it is now, and I am a gardener. I am a gardener *because* of her. I wander behind her as she moves from spot to spot, according to no plan anyone else can discern, weeding, deadheading, transplanting. I think she allows this because I live too far away to cramp her lone gardening style very often. Every once in a while, she even says something.

"This is gaillardia, but you know that," she says. "I love it, but I have trouble with it because it's easy. I can't grow anything easy."

Could this be why she gardens in West Gilgo Beach, where the native earth is nothing but wet sand, weeds, and scrubby pine trees? "Your grandmother always wanted to know how I could stand to break my back out here in this awful soil," Aunt Cookie remembers. "It might have been the challenge."

But it was also the memory of pre–World War Two tomatoes. My grandmother, apparently, was a sometime gardener, growing vegetables at their first summer home in Ridgefield, Connecticut. She sent Aunt Cookie out to weed, or to pick wild sorrel leaves with which to make the cold, sour, green Russian soup known as *stchav*. Aunt Cookie had no use for weeding or picking, but she always loved food.

"I used to take half a dozen tomatoes and a pot of salt to bed with me, and eat and read," Aunt Cookie recalls.

Then she skips from the 1930s, when the eating and reading began, to 1965, the year my grandfather died. "Someone sent a pot of tulips," she recalls. "I stuck them in the ground in a pot, out here in the sand.

Years later—about 1972—they suddenly began to bloom. And I bethought myself of the lovely homegrown tomatoes we used to eat. And I thought, 'Jeez, why can't *I* grow a good tomato?' "

It is just like Aunt Cookie to bethink herself when anyone else would just think; to begin to garden out of hunger for one good tomato; to plant those tulips in the first place. She could have thrown them away.

❦ ☀ ❦

My grandparents bought the West Gilgo Beach house in 1961. Aunt Cookie, Uncle Herb, and their daughter, Lisa, lived here with them every summer. Back then, the Chotzinoffs were not gardeners. I remember lots of music, poker, food, ocean, and conversation, not all of it in English. We were—and are—a family of incessant yakkers, equipped at birth with a full set of hair-trigger emotions. Between us, we have produced too much enthusiasm, anger, and hysterical laughter to fit between any four walls.

As a child, I came here with my father, Aunt Cookie's older brother, from our summer outpost further east in Hampton Bays, Long Island. My father instructed my sister, Jenny, and I to be firmly partial to *our* part of the island. West Gilgo, he said, was an unpleasant slab of gnatty sand and dune grass—hardly *More-Is-Better*. As if to rub it in, Aunt Cookie rewashed and reused plastic bags, hoarded cents-off coupons, and cooked gristly cuts of meat. Arguments about all that were an integral part of every family visit. Sometimes my father would storm off down the boardwalk, jaw clenched, suitcase in hand, Jenny and I tearing after him. Or we would continue to coexist for a few more days, except that several combinations of family members would be officially "not speaking." I liked it best when the snits gave way to some maniacal culinary project—like the time my Dad softened up a piece of raw abalone by driving his Impala over it, or the night Aunt Cookie tried to fry clams and they exploded all over the kitchen ceiling.

Explosions and Aunt Cookie are linked in my earliest memory: It is Sunday at 7 A.M. Lisa, Jenny, and I are playing a rousing (and fully costumed) game of Pirate on the living room furniture. Suddenly, Aunt Cookie appears at the top of the stairs, wearing a ratty bathrobe and a hairnet. Her eyes are slitty. "You sound like a herd of *elephants*," she yells.

Aunt Cookie also trounced us at jacks—which she played in a heel-squatting aboriginal stance—and snapped at us for grammatical transgressions, nose-picking, and failure to hold our stomachs in. But she also fed us Hebrew National hot dogs on sourdough bread and rare roast beef on pitas, and sometimes she allowed us full adult access to conversations about everything from crime to literature to sex.

So in West Gilgo, in the bosom of my family, I expect a full menu of mood swings. Around here, people are always bursting into song—bits of opera, bits of Cole Porter, bits of doggerel. Constant in-the-know references are made to all of literature—but that constitutes Calvin and Hobbes as well as Trollope. We are all snobs. We are all loons. We drive each other crazy.

You can flounder around for decades trying to hack out a niche of your own in a family like this. I like how Aunt Cookie has done it. At one time or another, she has been a writer, editor, translator of operas, TV and radio producer—and done all of it well. She says her life's work, in which she is now knee deep, is a translation of Verdi's *Falstaff*. I say it's gardening.

In the early summer of 1975, between high school and college, I was sent to kill time with Aunt Cookie and Uncle Herb because I didn't yet have a summer job. The visit turned sweet. I found three things to admire about Aunt Cookie.

1. She and Uncle Herb had a good marriage. They laughed often and conspiratorially. Every night, Aunt Cookie cooked something wonderful. Every night, Uncle Herb told her how wonderful it was, and then did all the dishes. They touched each other. They loved each other. All this is still true.

2. Aunt Cookie did not fuss with her looks. She was tall and lean, with short, brown, no-nonsense hair. In her closets hung fancy made-to-order evening clothes, but she walked around barefoot, her feet calloused, her knees scratched, the elastic in her bathing suits long since shot. She understood the comfort of old sweatshirts and sneakers worn into submission by salt air. I thought she was beautiful. All this is still true, too.

3. Aunt Cookie had a garden. It began to occur to me that gardening is the ultimate solitary pursuit, particularly for those who plan to grow old. There are no child prodigy gardeners. Gardeners are not "discovered." You really have no control over a garden. You may think you do, but you don't.

This, too, is still true, and I am still following Aunt Cookie in her garden.

I savor her running commentary: "This is called hesperis, I almost pulled it up and then something made me stop. The most long-lasting, wonderful flowers. It blooms in the spring, tra-la, and it likes the shade.

"This is a perennial lobelia, with a fascinating name, oh what is it?— a-ha! Syphilitica! Don't you like this salmony pink? I overplant like mad. I can't pay attention to that twelve-inch spacing because all I can think of is eleven inches of emptiness."

We step over the runners of wild cherry, around the thorns of the Fairy Rose, which roots here like a weed, and find ourselves in one of several vegetable outposts.

"EZ Pick beans. I used to grow all kinds. A French one. Kentucky Wonder. Blue Lake. Once, I threw them all into a pot and cooked them together, and it turns out there just ain't that much difference. Jerusalem artichokes. You have to restrain them scrupulously."

"And then you have to dig them up and scrub them for about three hours," I say.

"No, you clean them in the washing machine," Aunt Cookie replies. "Put them in a mesh bag, run them through the rinse cycle, pressure cook them, and puree them. Then stick them in the freezer and all summer long you'll have soup. Let's go look at my miserable little real artichoke."

There's just one, but it took her three years to grow. I'm impressed. She likes that. "I'm vain and I'm proud," she admits. We stroll past a rotted wooden catboat filled with potato vines. We pick blueberries and blackberries. We stop at a small pet cemetery covered with old roses and catnip. Uncle Herb appears on the deck outside the kitchen door—he's firing up the grill preparatory to cook a rack of spareribs. Tonight we'll have five different kinds of homegrown cherry and currant tomatoes, and coleslaw, but not from Aunt Cookie's cabbage.

"I did grow cabbage one dreadful year," she recalls. "The cabbage moths laid their rotten little eggs and that was the end of that. You see those sunburnt flowers coming down from the upstairs deck? I've always wanted nasturtiums to drape down. And I had some luck with Thompson and Morgan Starfire cascading marigolds. Right now the only thing cascading is me, from the heat."

Actually I've never known Aunt Cookie to fade, or even slow down, when it's humidly hot. She never could have imported these hundreds of yards of topsoil if she did. Because West Gilgo beach houses are accessible only by boardwalk and little red wagon, every single load of manure, salt hay, rotted leaves, and good dirt was trucked in, by Aunt Cookie and Uncle Herb, using either a wheelbarrow or brute strength. "I started with three forty-pound bags of topsoil," she recalls. "It seemed so monumental. It filled about like this," she says, indicating a plastic garbage can.

Before the massive dirt moving began, the neighbors had been happy with yards that consisted of little but sand. Once Aunt Cookie's garden got going, jealousy began to motivate them. The neighbors began planting their own flower beds, then tomatoes, then roses—and a network of plant trading and informed swiping began. All Aunt Cookie's azaleas, for instance, come from a neighbor who gets them from the window boxes at an East Village restaurant. If Aunt Cookie just happens to surreptitiously pinch cuttings at a nursery, a percentage of the resulting plants will be put into circulation.

"They call me the Heloise of the beach," she says. "People don't know how little I know. Sometimes I put something over on them. I like that," she admits. Which does not necessarily mean she has any desire to see what they've done with her information. "It depends," she says. "Something like Longwood Gardens, I'd love to see that. But going to visit gardens, that's different. There's always going to be something they do better than me, and that bothers me."

I started gardening ten years later than Aunt Cookie, and so far do nothing better. When she visits Denver, she gravitates to my backyard, and we compare notes on the intricacies of what she calls the "slobby garden" without the slightest competitive edge. Once, five years ago, we spent an afternoon searching my yard-high weeds for the Kentucky Wonder beans that had dried and turned into legumes. Aunt Cookie told me to put them in a mason jar, adding to my stash every time I weeded, "and then, around September," she said, "you can make wonderful soup."

Now, as dinner takes shape around me, I sit at this kitchen table reading back through Aunt Cookie's garden diaries, which she keeps meticulously each spring, but tapers off as harvests overwhelm her. It is not one of those how-the-plucky-squirrels-survive-winter accounts, nor does it rhapsodize much about any flower, even the rose. Spiritual growth is not a part of this narrative. In tone, it is realistically grumpy—sometimes even violent.

"Roses whacked back medium-hard," I read. "Added chicken shit. Triomphe de Farcy string bean not worth it. Sugar Ann not great. (Something) uprooted by vandals last night." At the beginning of a new season, however, I read this: "Tiny daffodil, what is it? It's adorable!" And later, in a different color pen, "oh! It's Minnow!"

Nowhere in these diaries are the emotions that lead Aunt Cookie into the garden, but she recently told me that they do—a fight with her husband, a fit of loneliness, a sense that "things are all ahoo." How, exactly, the act of pottering cures malaise she is unable to explain.

"It's very strange," she says. "I get terribly distracted. I wander around deadheading, planting this, planting that. I'm out there for a couple of hours, oh, at least. And if I think, I think very intensely and very intently about exactly what I'm doing. I try to think of more important things, but I can't."

☙ ☀ ❧

Although it was Aunt Cookie who taught me that you have less control over your garden than you think you do—and that the real rewards come from letting the garden control *you*—I still have the urge to break her style down into tiny pieces. We E-mail each other rigorously. I send specific questions—what do you wear in the garden? What's your idea of a perfect perennial bed? She answers expansively. Just today, I got this:

"I've seen many and many gorgeous gardens, some veddy formal, some slobby like mine (or yours), and I like most of them, but I don't think I'd want a perfect garden. My idea of a perfect garden is like a perfect house, one that's intensely personal, completely imperfect, if you get what I mean. For me a pleasing flower bed is a real mishmash of colors and shapes, with things like parsley and dill thrown in, and little hot peppers. I suppose what you'd call a cottage garden."

In midsummer, she writes of the joys of growing something nearly impossible, for the challenge:

"I'm intrigued by a highbush cranberry because I do not live in a bog (contrary to what your father thinks). And I passionately adore cranbs." As of yesterday, however, not a single berry has appeared. The coddled real artichoke, however, was harvested and tasted "absolutely terrible."

I ask for complaints and solutions to heat and bugs, and get them—Aunt Cookie obligingly bethinks herself of *The Children of Odin*, a mythology text, in which Loki, the Norse god of fire, is working at a forge to "work off a bet or something and the bad dwarf who has changed himself into a gadfly keeps buzzing him so that he can't keep the forge going evenly, and all Loki can do is shake his head and scream when he is being bitten. Bugs (mostly mosquitoes here, with an occasional infestation of black flies when there's a north or northwest wind) have been dreadful this year. We tried spraying the yard with Ivory dishwashing liquid through a hose-end sprayer, suggested by a neighbor. It works for about two hours and your garden smells awfully clean. Heat: I try to stay indoors from eleven to two or three. When desperate I jump in the ocean."

We air our reverse snobbism regarding gardening clothes. I tell her about my ancient skirted bathing suit.

"My favorite gardenwear," she replies, "is an old pair of Land's End pants called stringalongs. They have huge pockets for things like clippers and portable phones, and I'll die when they go. I feel that I look like a grungy country hick/scarecrow in the garden, especially if I'm wearing my falling apart straw flowerpot holder as a hat, and that's just fine with me."

Presumably, the fact that she can clearly be heard talking to herself while gardening is fine, too.

"When I pull up a good plant by mistake," she writes me at summer's end, "I say to myself Mr. Rochester's words after his marriage to Jane Eyre is interrupted: 'Jane, if a man had a lamb that was the love of his bosom and he sent it to the slaughter, he could not rue his bloody mistake more than I do.' That's if I pull a whole plant. If I cut the wrong flower, sometimes I say, 'Jane, I never meant to hurt you.' If it's only cutting a live bud when I'm deadheading, I just say 'Jane.' They know what I mean."

Deadheading is just the kind of thing I don't do often or well enough, but lately I have achieved a sort of truce with it. My mind goes blank, and sometimes I even say "Jane." That's when I bethink myself of Aunt Cookie, and miss her, and wish I were about to eat anything at all she grows, even the terrible-tasting artichoke. Whenever I feel this way, I search the shed for a Ziploc bag full of screened compost from Aunt Cookie's oldest heap. I asked her for it and she gave it to me. She did not consider it an odd request.

Aunt Cookie's Recipe
❧ for a Nice Bowl of Stchav ❧

Buy some stchav in a bottle. (I've had best luck and by far best price with Gold's; Rokeach tends to be stringy; Mother's is pricey but good.) Dice one medium/large peeled cucumber, put on paper towel to drain, chop up two or three scallions, all the green and most of the white, mash them in a bowl with salt, probably half a teaspoon. Put in several heaping tablespoons of sour cream. This year I use $^1/_3$ real, $^1/_3$ light, and $^1/_3$ Dannon No-Fat Yogurt. Add a few tablespoons of the soup and stir till no more sour cream lumps, keep adding and stirring. Get very cold (soup, not you). You can add a few ice cubes. Mix in cucumber and serve in cold bowls.

7 Tomatoes

The street fills up with tomatoes,
mid-day,
summer,
the light divides the tomato in two halves,
the juice runs down the streets.

In December the tomato breaks loose,
it invades the kitchens
entering through lunch,
it sits,
resting on the sideboards,
among the glasses,
the butter dishes,
the blue salt cellars . . .

PABLO NERUDA, "ODA AL TOMATE"

Nothing, nothing, nothing tastes like a ripe tomato you grew yourself, eaten on the evening of a day so hot there can be no question of even a nip of spring or fall.

One such evening in the middle of a dinner party, I went back to the garden to harvest another dozen ears of sweet corn, which my guests were eating raw off the cob. I was wearing a long dress and bare feet. My good horse-poop-strengthened soil crumbled between my toes. A man walking by in the alley said: "Is that your garden? Christ, it looks like the Mexican jungle."

I took this as a compliment, for my garden had reached the midsummer abandon stage with a wonderful zeal that year. Seen from a rusted metal lawn chair, it was densely wild, with pumpkin vines underfoot and volunteer marigolds giving off their potent pollen scent. All around it was a stockade of Jerusalem artichokes. The Japanese eggplant hung from their small bushes like heavy earrings; the bell peppers were turning red. This is exactly right, I thought—and in the next breath, naturally, perversely, I began to imagine living without it. While doing so, I ate tomatoes.

I ate a deep red Beefmaster, an acid yellow Lemon Boy, a bland American Better Boy, and a small nosegay of purple basil. I could live without lettuce, cutting flowers, baby carrots, or the corn I'd come to pick in the first place, but never without tomatoes.

In winter, I daydream of tomatoes sliced onto a fish-shaped glass plate and sprinkled with olive oil and basil. I compare the warm slurp of a real tomato to the evil, spongy, pinkish, watery Safeway version. And I admire its willingness. Every single year my tomatoes are subjected to hailstorms, hornworms, and verticillium wilt, which is when you're supposed to uproot the plants and destroy them. But I never do, because even sick tomato plants still give tomatoes. Finally, though it is all too easy to feel like hell on a clear summer day—easier than in a fall rain, which seems to sympathize—it is nearly impossible to despair while eating my own tomato, outside, with my bare feet in dirt.

I love tomatoes. I am not alone, of course.

∽ ☀ ∼

"To eat three or four tomatoes one after the other," Bill Palmer muses. "To *lust* after the taste. To take a really sharp knife with long, thin teeth and slice them thin, about a quarter inch, with a knife that slices like paper. To me, that tastes better than to just chomp down and let it squirt all over the place. You can't buy the taste," he concludes. "You really can't *buy* a tomato."

This is the easy explanation for why Bill has 450 tomato plants this year—down from last year's all-time high of one thousand. This is why his North Boulder yard, eight-tenths of an acre in size and choked with long grass, overgrown weeds, and unkempt scrap trees, is so different than those of his neighbors, who are upwardly mobile in the classic, carpet-of-green-lawn-edged-with-marigolds way.

"I'm striving toward perfection," is how Bill explains it. He hasn't made the comparison between his yard and the others. He's not interested. He's not interested in *any* yards that don't contain tomatoes. "I liken it to wine," he says. "I can tell the different tomato varieties by taste alone. I'm Don Quixote. If one out of all my plants turns out perfect, that's all I want."

Bill began gardening here ten years ago, before the houses tripled in value. He dug irrigation ditches, uprooted trees, and built tomato cages from concrete reinforcing wire. Each year, in mid-January, he starts seeds for up to a hundred varieties of tomato. He's had brief flirtations with flowers and other, lesser, vegetables, but tomatoes are his obsession.

"I even have wild dreams of building a public tomato garden here in Boulder," he says. "There would be so much bounty. People could eat whatever they wanted."

There is some question as to whether Bill himself would frequent such a place. He is an intensely private man, forty-seven, slightly built, with brown hair turning gray and brown eyebrows still brown. A divorced father of three, he lives with all three kids as well as his ailing father—yet his house, surrounded as it is by tomatoes and underbrush, has an uninhabited look. And though he agrees to show me the garden, he later requests that we meet to talk about it "on neutral ground. Perhaps the library." Finding the time, he adds, will be tough, because he plays Scrabble for a living and is out of town more than he'd like. Later, he

120

amends that to say that "certain investments" have paid off well enough that he doesn't really have to work, but that he enjoys Scrabble enough to play the circuit.

"I couldn't really do all this if I had to punch the clock," he says thoughtfully. Has he ever? He sidesteps the question by saying, "You're right about hands. Mine get so dirty in summer I can't even get them clean with bleach, and I *won't* wear gloves."

Dirt was Bill's love long before he fell for plants. "When I was about ten," he recalls, "my mother had a house on the Massachusetts coast. I cleared out a whole half acre of back lot. There were lots of old trees and brambles. It was important for me to do it because everyone said I couldn't."

It wasn't until 1984 that Bill first planted tomatoes in the ground he cleared. He longed for the taste, he says, but there were mental benefits, too.

"Gardening is all the things I'm not," he says. "It's patient. A garden has a vision and it's hard for me to find my visions. In a garden, you get *involved* in time, there's no time pressure, there's always next year. And even when I've planted hundreds of plants by myself, it's not hard work. It's flowing work. People could have a field day analyzing what's going on here. We could go back to my childhood and probably find something."

Bill stops talking abruptly. He doesn't want to revisit his childhood. So we visit the garden, where the tomato plants are crammed in rows of twenty, the shoulders of their cages touching. The fence that surrounds Bill's property has been reinforced with old slabs of plywood, bales of hay, extra layers of barbed wire—anything to keep out the deer, which, in this rapidly gentrifying neighborhood, know an herbaceous playground when they see it. Seen from the fence, Bill's place looks like a cross between a prison camp and the set from *Hee-Haw*.

"It makes no difference to the deer," Bill says. "They just jump right over and eat. I could spray the plants with hot sauce. I could work harder on the fence. I will overcome this with measured action, even though my tendency is to flare."

"What do you mean, *flare?*" I ask. "Is it that you really want to *shoot* a deer?"

"Ha," Bill says morosely. "If I murdered someone, I might get two years. But around here, if I killed a deer, I'd be lynched."

Luckily, however, with 450 tomato plants, enough fruit survives. "I am very behind in the marketing end," Bill confesses. "I have thought of selling these tomatoes or bringing them to the farmer's market, but I don't."

"What happens to them?"

"I eat two to three pounds a day, every day, from June through September."

"What about the rest of them?"

"They rot. I need to find a vision about that."

At this point, I begin eating tomatoes as fast as I can. Boulder's weather is markedly more volatile than Denver's—though the two towns are separated by just thirty-six miles—and a rogue frost could set in any time. Besides, I'm not sure I've ever eaten my fill of tomatoes.

Among the varieties I taste are Pappy's Feast, a sweet pink tomato bred in the mountains of West Virginia; Evergreen, which is disconcertingly green, but tastes red; and Garden Lime, which Bill describes as "a brownish, yellowish green." Like a bruise, I think, but it has the taste Bill loves—sweet, as opposed to acid, with lots of seeds and pulp. The only familiar tomato I come across is Sungold, the hybrid yellow-red cherry Aunt Cookie grows (and eats) by the bushel.

"I suppose I could grow Fantastik and Celebrity," Bill reflects, "but Celebrity is an all-season radial tire of a tomato and I am concerned only with taste."

And on this subject, he is fanatic. "You *must* pick before the sun comes up," he tells me. "Eaten in the afternoon, tomatoes are only five percent as good. You should pick them at 5:00 A.M. Every hour they sit around picked, they lose flavor."

This may be technically true, but shouldn't a garden tomato be warm with sun when you pick it? And 5:00 A.M. seems a cold hour.

"Maybe," Bill says, "but some of my most sublime moments have been at four in the morning when the irrigation water comes through. Alone, under the full moon, in the garden, you see subtle variations. Sometimes I look at the foliage of my tomatoes and think I would grow tomatoes even if they didn't grow fruit. It's like looking at the stars as your eyes become accustomed to the dark. First you see a thousand stars, then you see ten thousand."

✿ ☼ ✿

In the early spring of 1980, I dug up my first vegetable garden in the yard of a rental house, using a tiny folding camping spade. I went to the

122

Ace Hardware and bought ten seed packets, among them tomatoes and zucchini. I tried measuring careful rows with stakes and string, but when that grew dull, I scattered the seed anywhere. Three months went by, during which a lot of weeds grew and I was too distracted to pull them. Besides, I'd been told by then that you can't plant tomatoes from seed in Colorado, especially not in April, before the last frost. Imagine my surprise in late September when I discovered a massive crop of medium, round tomatoes crowded under a mat of weeds.

But tomatoes are like that. They are always doing something dramatic. My favorite tomato story comes from my friend Brian Gaffney, who worked off his college summers in a sewage treatment plant in Mendham, New Jersey.

"It was a really old, really lousy plant," he told me. "The sewage wasn't enclosed like it is today. So all this human waste would flow through a sort of cement-lined river, and at one point it actually hit a fan. And the fan would fling particles into the air, and they would land in the grass. And in that grass grew some of the largest, most beautiful tomato plants anyone had ever seen. And no one would touch them."

❦ ☀ ❧

I am starting to feel hardened toward weird, showboat tomatoes, when I come face to face with Black Krim, the Soviet tomato. A good pound in weight, its skin grayish black, its flesh overripe to the touch, it is about as attractive as pond scum. I pick one anyway and take a big bite, letting the juice and black seeds run down my chin.

"Not bad, huh," says Keith Slocum. "We have quite a few Russian tomatoes, actually. They like tomatoes over there."

This works for Keith, whose two-year-old company, Seeds By Design, produces exotic and heirloom tomatoes for seed, selling them to seed brokers all over the world. Keith and I are walking through an eight-acre plot he leased this year and planted in long rows of tomatoes interspersed with low hedges of lemon basil. The mix of herb and ripe tomato smells like summer itself.

"When you drive north from Sacramento," Keith told me on the phone, "keep coming north till it looks like you're right up against the hills. And that's because you will be."

So I'm about thirty-five miles northeast of Chico, California, in a wide, gentle valley where the climate is unsurpassedly hospitable to tomatoes. I've been driving through old farm towns where palm trees line the sidewalks but snow can be seen on the mountain tops. Between plane time and car time, I've been sitting down for six hours. Now I get to spend the rest of the day walking down long rows of tomato plants, feeling the fertile air on my skin and eating tomatoes.

For a while, we just stand still, absorbing the late sun and breathing in basil. A powerfully built man in his late thirties, Keith has darkly tanned arms, but his face, shaded by a wide-brimmed felt hat, is pale. He looks like your basic John Steinbeck–model California farmer, but he isn't. Having spent most of his life selling seed for much bigger companies than this, he's just beginning to understand the more mechanical tools of the ag trade. He doesn't own this field. It belongs to a local grower, who's contracted with Seeds By Design to raise the tomatoes. All summer, Keith's been coming by to check up on the crop— and this is just one of eight similar fields located in the surrounding forty miles—but it's only in the past week that he's actually had to do hands-on work with the tomatoes. Migrant crews are arriving to harvest and process the fruit, and Keith, who only recently figured it out himself, has had to show them how it's done. On the dirt road below us, a huge tractor waits to be driven to a barn and rinsed out.

I've never been this close to a tractor before. Keith asks if I would like to drive it. With a great grinding of gears, the tractor lurches forward, under my command. It's like rolling a grand piano down a hill.

"I'm sure one of these levers is a brake," Keith says helpfully. "But I forgot how to use this thing. I just borrowed it, actually."

Fifteen minutes later we arrive at a field where a crew of workers is reducing a field of cherry tomatoes to foamy slop. The two Spanish-speaking men running the futuristic tractor attachment are sticky with tomato juice, and the ground for yards around is covered with a flat pink puddle, inside of which wasps are dying of gluttony. After sitting for two days in rubber garbage cans so that they can float loose from the placenta of tomato pulp, the seeds will be spread out to dry, sewn into canvas bags, and sent away—anywhere from Saudi Arabia to the Midwest.

"Tomorrow we'll do the Pink Oxhearts for a company in Wisconsin," Keith tells me. "They seem to like that pink color." He picks me one from the long row of plants. It's almost triangular in shape, and its taste is acid and overflowing, just the way I like it.

"The Latin name for this tomato is, oh hell, I don't remember," Keith says. "You should see me trying to write descriptions of these seeds. I mean, how many times can you say *looks good, tastes great?* But it's amazing what WordPerfect can do when I run out of adjectives."

In any case, this being the height of the growing season, he hasn't sat at a desk for months. When he does, he says, it's mostly "pink, creamy, indeterminate" or "large beefsteak, matures seventy days." Unless he's describing something larger than life—like Radiator Charlie's Mortgage Lifter. We're walking through a row of it right now.

"Try it," Keith urges, trying one himself. It's a light red, *big* tomato, with the kind of lumpy shoulders characteristic of older tomato types. It would taste great, I think, with a big slab of bacon and some rye bread. "Mortgage Lifter was developed in the twenties by this radiator repairman," Keith explains. "He sold the plants for a dollar each, and they did so well he paid off his mortgage."

Following Radiator Charlie, which I agree is a star, I sample Gardener's Delight, which Keith calls "the best-tasting indeterminate cherry around"; Atkinson, the quintessential medium red eating tomato; Angora, named for its fuzzy leaves; and Potato Leaf Orange, which Keith admits "tastes awful—but so what. It makes a beautiful patio plant." I am vaguely repulsed by the taste of Caro Rich, with its violently orange fruit—and then I remember that this is the only tomato Bill Palmer freezes. ("It assumes the texture of a popsicle," he told me, "but you still get that sweet aftertaste. It's better than nothing.")

Soon I am taking just one bite out of each tomato and flinging away the rest. At the end of this hedonistic tour, my favorite tomato is Brandywine, and its cousin Yellow Brandywine. Both are old, with lumpy asymmetrical shapes, have a tendency to grow very large, and are faintly striped when you cut them open. Their taste is slightly lemon and very beefy.

At the end of the row, Keith's business partner, Patty Buskirk, waits with unsettling news. "The Navajos never got their onion seed," she says flatly. "They got lettuce instead."

A conversation full of inside references to the intricacies of plant breeding and shipping ensues—complete with dark allusions to a much larger rival seed company. Since I can't understand a word of it, I take a good look at Patty. She resembles a young—and vastly pregnant—Debbie Reynolds.

"Here's how it works at Seeds By Design," she says. "Keith's the dreamer, I'm the realist. There isn't anything he won't try. Now me, I was raised on a hundred-and-fifty-acre almond ranch in a teeny tiny town near here. When you had to get something done, you got it done."

Patty has always known exactly what she wanted to do with her life, starting with the certainty that she is "an outdoors person. I do not like to be inside a house, even a nice house, and that is why my house is terribly messy." At sixteen, she found work as a plant breeder's helper, assisting with pollinations, then she studied for a bachelor's degree in agriculture at Chico State University. "I was a half semester short, but I went to work for Northrup-King anyway," she tells me. As a plant breeder, she focused her talent on squash, which she loves to distraction. "I don't care much for tomatoes," she adds. I find this hard to believe. "Never eat 'em," she confirms. "Now a good squash, a Burgess butternut, that sucker will *produce*. If you really want something to write about, you should come out and see some squash."

Patty and Keith met while working at a local company called Western Seed—he as a salesman and she as a plant breeder. After they became friends, it occurred to both of them that the world of established seed wholesalers had grown stagnant.

"What I wanted to do was play around with heritage seeds, unusuals, herbs," Keith recalls. "I saw all the other companies getting deeper and deeper into hybrids with no flavor. I knew I was going in the opposite direction. Every time I'd get some of the heritage seeds produced, I'd sell out so quickly. Now a tomato like Celebrity, it's okay, it's a workhorse—but a two-pound striped tomato, that's something to care about."

Two years ago, Seeds By Design entered the market with a line of little-known seeds Keith and Patty collected from seed savers and plant breeders all over the United States. Though they offer everything from herbs to asparagus, their primary focus is on tomatoes—despite Patty's distrust of them. "We have forty-five varieties, mostly heirloom, all wonderful," Keith says.

"So you still eat tomatoes?" I ask him.

"Oh, I go through three, four buckets of tomatoes just to sun-dry each fall," he says. "I cut up Romas and lay them out on screens. In the winter, I put them on pizza, and I remember."

"They smell like they *eat* wonderful," Patty says, trying to understand.

"But it's not just that," Keith insists. "It's gardening. It makes me feel good, and it's good for me, and there's a difference. There's plenty things that make you feel good and are not good for you at all. Try this Amana Orange," he says, handing me a fat, warm, bright orange fruit. "It's a

Mennonite tomato. Oh, it's a good one."

I bite in. He's right.

⊂ ☀ ⊃

I do not have room for forty-five varieties of heirloom tomatoes, let alone 450. I can accommodate three plants, none of them prima donnas. This year I grew: Celebrity (the old workhorse), Lemon Boy (my favorite acid yellow), and Big Rainbow, a Seeds By Design heirloom that grows large and striped. It's a little too sweety-sweety in taste for me, but I grew it because it's big. Big tomatoes impress me. Sometimes, while standing around with my tomatoes, I fantasize about growing a tomato as large as a human head.

Why? Well, perhaps there are two kinds of gardeners. Some care for the effete things—flavor, appearance, and rarity. But maybe the rest of us are genetically programmed to strive for prizes at county fairs. Perhaps, in a past life, I was a 4-H guest lecturer. I believe a tomato should be weighty.

When you set out to grow a huge tomato, the first two words that should occur to you are *Miracle* and *Gro*. All you have to do is listen to a day's worth of talk radio, and you will understand the deeply symbiotic relationship between the Stearns Miracle-Gro fertilizer company and a certain class of people whose only aim in life is to grow enormous vegetables. When it comes to tomatoes, once you've surpassed the two-pound mark, you should give Miracle-Gro a call. They want to hear from you.

"I've spent this whole growing season talking to people who grow big vegetables," says Jolee Dunham, a P.R. agent for B. L. Ochman and Company, the New York City firm that represents Miracle-Gro. "I am in touch with these weird people like you wouldn't believe. I know all about the deaths in their family, their freaky, freaky accidents, and, of course, their tomatoes."

This is not just because Miracle-Gro likes to use actual customers in their TV and print ads, but because, for the past two years, it's been running a high-profile tomato contest.

"There's a hundred thousand dollars at stake," Jolee says. "The point is to beat Gordon Graham. In 1987, Gordon got the Guinness record with a seven-pound-twelve-ounce tomato. He's a housepainter and he lives in Edmond, Oklahoma. His garden is magnificent. He could put sticks in the ground and they would grow."

127

Miracle-Gro is so impressed with Gordon Graham, Jolee says, that they pay his expenses whenever he wants to do anything remotely garden-related. They ship him hundred-pound boxes of fertilizer. They use him in ads, "and he is wonderful," Jolee says. "He looks just like an extra out of *Deliverance*."

But all through the summer of 1994, she also kept strict tabs on anyone anywhere else in the country who might be coming close to breaking the record. In early October, she sent me a list of more than fifty gardeners she'd been chatting with almost weekly. One of them was 63-year-old Minnie Zacaria of Long Branch, New Jersey, who's had the annual New Jersey Championship Tomato Weigh-In sewed up for more than a decade, but will not rest until she wins the Miracle-Gro title as well.

"I think there wasn't a sport I didn't go out for as a girl," Minnie tells me over the phone. "I move fast, I move athletic. If you saw me, you'd never think I was a grandmother."

Even if I did, I wouldn't want to compete with her—in tomatoes, or anything else. Minnie's gardening obsession is fueled by bold-faced jealousy and the urge to win.

"When I was very young," she recalls, "my father had tomatoes, that's all he grew, and I knew I could do it. I sent for a package of any old seeds, started them in old containers with no drainage holes, and planted them in a bare spot in the lawn. They sprouted and died and that was my beginning. After I got married I started to bone up on it a little, got my own garden and my own yard."

She was just starting to feel cocky when an "old-timer" of the old-school, Italian-American variety came by and laughed at her tomatoes. "He told me, if I wanted to see *real* tomatoes, I should look at his. He said my tomatoes were puny and oh, he made fun of me," Minnie says, still irked, "and that's what started my devotion. I started sneaking by his house to look at his tomatoes. I wouldn't give him the satisfaction of visiting during the daylight hours."

For the next twenty years, Minnie slaved away, doing everything she could to produce "bigger and better tomatoes." In 1981, the year she first produced a three-pounder, she came in sixth in the New Jersey tomato weigh-in. The next year, she crossbred her own giant tomato seed—which she calls 'Big Zack', and will not sell for love or money— and won a $500 runner-up prize. "I was the only female that entered," she recalls proudly. "The women were out of the running completely."

She took first prize the next five years in a row—but by then, she had her sights set on Gordon Graham's record.

"I mean, what is that tomato, a freak of nature?" she frets."I mean, excuse me, but they don't always check, and I kind of doubt the Guinness book. I've never seen a picture of that seven-pound-twelve-ounce tomato. I do a four-pound tomato every year and it's not easy. You have to know what you're doing, I don't care who you are."

Minnie produced a four-and-a-half-pound tomato during the 1994 season. It was enough to earn her several long, intimate phone calls with Jolee Dunham, as well as all the free fertilizer she could use, but it didn't even approach Gordon Graham's record.

Meanwhile, in the mountainous town of St. Clairsville, Ohio, a retired baker named Robert Ehigh was coming very, very close.

"I been gardening all my life, always tomatoes," Ehigh says, "but to tell you the truth, I don't really know why they went ape this year. My ground here is not worth a durn. It's full of lime. Maybe," he muses, "it's because we have The Seed."

Robert won't even give The Seed a name—"some company would pester me to buy it"—but here's its story. Robert's wife's grampa developed it more than forty-five years ago, as best as anyone in St. Clairsville can remember. "When he passed away, he had them seeds in a little medicine bottle, and no one even knew what vegetable they were for," Robert recalls. "I planted them and, my Lord, they came up real good, meaty, not too acidy, somewhere in between yellow and reddish. And big! A sort of West Virginia hillbilly tomato. They gave me three-pound tomatoes without even trying and that was before this year, when they went ape."

Late this spring, Ehigh noticed that one of his plants had developed a stem "as big around as a broom handle." Only one tomato was growing from it, and it looked enormous. That's when, having heard about the beat-Gordon-Graham contest, he called Miracle-Gro. They sent him a check for a hundred bucks and a whole lot of fertilizer and told him to stay in touch.

"By August," Jolee Dunham remembers, "we sent a guy from the local extension out to weigh Robert's tomato on the vine. Best we could tell, it had to be six-and-a-quarter pounds. And we started the watch. Robert had been sitting out there with a shotgun and we told him to go get some sleep. We hired round-the-clock armed guards for him."

"Then I sat in the house answering the telephone," Robert

remembers. "I don't know how, but everyone had heard of my tomato. The guards were outside sitting under the apple tree, to keep these smart kids from trying to get The Seed. I had a little tent rigged up over Baby"—his affectionate name for the six-pounder—"and a sling holding it up. We had the radio on playing old hillbilly music, and Baby seemed to like that."

Miracle-Gro even sent Gordon Graham to visit. He made no suggestions, other than recommending that Robert Ehigh switch from hillbilly music to country and western, which Robert promptly did—though he snuck in Frank Sinatra from time to time. By mid-September, Baby was big enough to qualify as a media event.

"Robert's garden had become a sort of pilgrimage place," Jolee says. "People heard about it on Paul Harvey and just came on over. And Baby kept gaining weight. We figured it was way over seven pounds."

A few phone calls later, all the New York morning shows—from *Good Morning America* to *Today*—were vying for tomato-weighing rights. "We gave it to *Regis and Kathie Lee*, because right at that moment we were supposed to invade Haiti," Jolee recalls. "Regis and Kathie Lee do not bump tomato guests for invasions. So we flew Robert and his wife and Baby, each on their own first-class seat, to New York."

They were destined for great, if momentary, fame—followed by even greater disappointment.

"Baby got rotten on me, to tell you the truth," Robert says. "We left her on the vine too long—long enough for the *National Enquirer* to take a picture—and it was getting those cracks on it. The day we was on television, it actually had mold on it."

"That, or too many people touched it," Jolee says. "It got a hole in it and sprung a leak like you had turned on a faucet. We kept having to change the tablecloth underneath it and it only weighed out at four pounds, five ounces." Miracle-Gro extended the contest through fall of 1995, and gave Robert Ehigh a $10,000 consolation check for being a good sport.

Robert says he plans to "demolish" the money by purchasing new rugs and windows—and he certainly has no hard feelings. "I would never want to drive a car in New York City," he says, "but what a time we had! They had what you call a greenroom, where we sat around eating sweet rolls and everything."

"Well now, a lot of it is luck," says Gordon Graham, who has stayed in touch with Robert Ehigh since the *Regis and Kathie Lee* debacle. "I don't feel *good* about old Robert losing, if that's what you think. I remember when Miracle-Gro asked, just kind of friendly-like, what I thought of someone growing a bigger one. I says flat out: *It's not gonna be long before someone does.*"

But even Gordon himself hasn't managed to exceed four pounds since his 1987 behemoth. "Tomatoes have just been my hobby and fascination for so many years, and I'm fifty-seven now," he tells me by phone. "I'd always read the Guinness book and I decided to grow the tallest tomato plant in the world. I grew a fifty-two-footer nine years ago, and broke the record, but everyone said you can't do that again, it was just luck. So I dug a hole three feet deep and threw in everything— compost, perlite, vermiculite—and planted a Delicious tomato. It got up about twelve feet high and fell over on my cantaloupe patch, and I quit fertilizing and forgot all about it."

In late September that year, while harvesting melon, Gordon says he lifted up a cantaloupe vine and found the world-famous tomato sitting there on a bed of straw, undiscovered by birds or hornworms. It was unheard-of luck, he says. It may never be equaled again. Meanwhile, Gordon is a celebrity for the duration.

"People from California and New York stop by here all the time," he says. "Even some from England. I don't try to be famous, but the local papers play it up. They think it's kind of cute."

"Has all this ruined tomatoes for you?" I ask.

"Why, the tomato is the number one vegetable grown in the world," Gordon says indignantly. "Of course I still love tomatoes. I plant sixty, seventy plants every year, and sometimes I sit out there till twelve or one in the morning, just enjoying them and looking up at the stars. It's a wonderful time to talk to yourself."

"What about?"

"I don't mean to sound religious," he says, "but I usually thank God for everything he's given me. I talk about the bond between the earth and soil and spirituality. And I think about pumpkins, too," he says.

"Pumpkins?"

"I belong to the World Pumpkin Confederation," he explains. "We're striving for a thousand-pound pumpkin. It's something to think about. Not that it compares to a tomato," he adds.

What does?

Gordon Graham's
✺ Favorite Big Tomato Varieties ✺

Brandywine

German Johnson

Radiator Charlie's Mortgage Lifter

Giant Belgian

Park's Whopper

✺ Bill Palmer's Crucial Tomato Tip ✺

Manipulate nature by five degrees at night. If you can get the temperature in your tomato bed from 58 degrees up to 63, it's like you moved your garden seven hundred miles south.

8 Natives

*See, I think this land
will change you.
I don't think outsiders have been
able to change it as much as
they thought they had.*

ED CASTILLO IN 500 NATIONS,
BY ALVIN M. JOSEPHY, JR.

"They say we've been here since 1043," says Elizabeth Haile. "There's carbon dating. That's one thing. But we've always been here. We just know it."

She folds her hands and smiles at us. We are sitting in folding chairs arranged in a semicircle—an official tour group, all paying polite attention. "We've always been here," Elizabeth repeats. "And today you're on our land, and you're welcome."

Her land is eight-hundred acres of reservation on eastern Long Island, where the Shinnecock Indians have lived since 1704. It is the oldest Indian reservation in the country, and, as far as I can tell, one of the most private. Few of the Indians I know in Denver have ever heard of it. And even though I spent sixteen summers within a mile of this place, I've never been inside it until now.

Elizabeth Haile has dressed for the occasion in what she calls her "regalia," though it's low key compared to what she wears at the Shinnecock's annual Labor Day Powwow. On her feet are handmade deerskin moccasins; on her body a green *muumuu* sewn with beads. If there is an Indian way for a person to look, she does—her face is round, with wide cheekbones, and her hair is long, straight, and black. "But that's because I dye it," she tells me later. "I'm actually almost seventy years old, but you can't tell, can you?"

Outside, it's a typical early August day—humid and hazy, with no wind. The building where we sit is spare and cool inside, with basketball hoops at either end and a kitchen and tribal offices along its west side. Other than a few posters featuring native actors advising Indian youth to stay off drugs and alcohol, the only decoration is the design of a huge wampum belt painted on the white walls.

Yesterday's tour group consisted of Pequot Indians from Connecticut, and the official presentation gave way to something rowdy and fun. Today's group is more staid—three instructors from a Manhattan Parks Department program, fifteen of their student/cadets, and me. Until this summer, it has not been the Shinnecock way to bring people from outside onto the reservation—except at powwow time. But this has been a season of official lectures and presentations. Without them, says Elizabeth, there would be no way to support the Shinnecock Nation Cultural Center/Museum.

"We are trying to gather our past," she explains. "We have decided to interpret our own history. These young people who are working on it, they believe in practicality. Nobody around here is really interested in dry bones or arrowhead collections. What we want to show is the way we once lived. So we are going to show you our garden."

In years to come, the garden will be the centerpiece of the Shinnecock's living museum, which will be open to paying customers from outside. But it's Shinnecock children, Elizabeth says, who really need to see it. "We have to show our young people, before they forget entirely what it means to be part of an Indian family," she says. "Right now, they get past the first two pages of social studies, and they're done with Indians. We have to say: *you better read those pages carefully.*"

What visitors to the Cultural Center/Museum see this summer is not a building or a display case but Elizabeth Haile, who tells them what is to come, and the beginnings of the garden. "We're taking seeds from the old forms of vegetables and propagating them and teaching the use of those foods," she says. "We have begun to grow ancient vegetables. The kind you don't find in a supermarket."

One of the parks department instructors raises his hand: "So were you hunter-gatherers, or what?" he asks.

This is the kind of question Elizabeth, who comes alive in front of a crowd, loves.

"Oh, we hunted and gathered everything in sight," she begins. "We farmed the land and we farmed the sea. Our life was circular. The human being is only one element of life—there are also the things that swim, the things that fly in the sky, those that grow out of the earth, the four-legged creatures, and, finally, the two-leggeds, the humans. As two-leggeds, we are only entitled to just so much."

"Oh," the instructor says. "What I meant was, what kind of stuff did you eat and where did you get it?"

Elizabeth replies that long ago, the Shinnecocks fished from dugout canoes and grew corn, which they stored in cellar holes.

"So you guys don't go to the supermarket?" asks a cadet, who is not too sure when *long ago* was.

"No," Elizabeth says patiently. "We are dependent on that just like everyone else. But now, we are beginning to eat some of what we always ate. Corn, beans, and squash. We like to say," she begins, the public-speaking look creeping over her face, "that corn is tallest sister, and she grew straight up to the sun. The second sister, beans, grew winding up the first sister. And the third sister—that is squash—grew low and broadly to keep the weeds down."

♋ ☀ ♋

It's seven miles from Hampton Bays to Southampton on the Montauk Highway. As a child, I sat through this drive countless times, always taking note of the Plains Indian tepee outside the Shinnecock's highway gift shop. As I grew older, I noticed first one, then two discount cigarette stores.

I was curious. Our family summer house sat on the shores of Shinnecock Bay, we fished from the rocks of Shinnecock Inlet—once, in winter, we even stayed at a Shinnecock Motel—but that one word was all I knew about the local Indians, even as I raided the Hampton Bays Public Library for children's books on the romantic Sioux and Cheyenne. It was weird.

Weirder still was the fact that no one I asked knew anything about the Shinnecock Indians—and some people I asked were descendants of families who had shared this land with Indians for more than three-hundred years. My family never went to the Labor Day Powwow, because, my Dad said, it was crowded and touristy. Besides, he already had a Shinnecock story to tell. Once, while sailing on Shinnecock Bay, he beached on reservation land, and was met by a tall black man who calmly said "How." That, right there, was the one item in circulation about the Shinnecocks: Because they intermarried with black slaves hundreds of years ago, you really couldn't tell them apart. They might, I heard, not be "real Indians" anymore. Later, I read this in a locally written book of Hampton Bays history, along with the commonly held view that "Shinnecock women make excellent housekeepers and nurses."

If I had wanted to investigate this claim—or if I had wanted to find out what all Shinnecock men excel at, for that matter—it would have been difficult. You don't just pop in to visit the Shinnecock Indians. Their land, which butts up against the ritz of Southampton, has a similar air of zealously protected privacy. But where the million-dollar

137

Southampton summer houses are screened by privet hedges and driveways that curve just enough to keep you from seeing anything, the Shinnecock are not as coy. If you try to visit their reservation, you will run smack into a sign telling you to keep out.

"Yes, we're private," Elizabeth Haile tells me. "But we're like any other species that way. If you walk along a country road and you see two pheasant, that means there are twenty—eighteen you *can't* see. That's Shinnecock."

As I walk along Church Street on the way to the Shinnecock garden, I see simple frame houses with cedar shingles—smaller, but otherwise similar to many on eastern Long Island. All the houses are set in fields of grass with windbreak trees at their edges. I don't see a petunia or a daisy, let alone a full-fledged garden. I've been told that this tribe, once expert growers of maize, have forgotten how to garden. I've also been told the garden they started last year is skimpy at best—but I already like the thought of it, because I think the Shinnecock's desire to relearn what they once knew about their land is honorable. Also, when it comes to gardening, none of us are experts.

Looking around, I see no *us*. The street is empty of anyone but the tour group and Gerrod Smith, project director for the Cultural Center. He is a short, strong man, thirty-nine years old, with straight black hair worn in a braid, a bandanna tied around his forehead, and the kind of reddish skin that must have given rise to the term. He wears what he wears every day regardless of the heat—long pants, a western shirt, heavy work boots. Because he's always dressed for hacking through the underbrush, and because he'd rather do that than sit at his desk writing grant proposals, his friends call him Bush Man. His looks are pure ethnicity. His accent is pure Long Island.

"I guess you know this is the black cherry," he says, beginning an informal talk on medicinal plants, herbs, and weeds. "You can cook it, and make a kind of saucy berry dessert thing."

We walk single file into a field of waist-high weeds, which breaks into a clearing containing a garden and the start of a Shinnecock village, circa 1043. There is the skeleton of a wickiup, framed from bent saplings tied together with cattails and covered with birch bark mats; a mortar and pestle made by dropping a coal into the hollow of a stump and letting it burn into a bowl; and clamshell scrapers for curing deer hides.

While Gerrod talks about weeds, I walk into the garden. The twenty-by-forty-foot plot is bare in the middle, with stands of corn on either end. The soil is light, light brown, and seems impoverished. Around the edges of the tilled land are weeds; in and among the corn stalks are smaller plants I can't identify, except for purple feathers of amaranth. Are these ancient vegetables? Is this how it looked before the first white people landed on Long Island, some twenty miles away?

Gerrod says all he knows is that his brother, Lamont, has been talking to Seed Savers, the Decorah, Iowa, repository, for years—and that this is as close to the original Shinnecock garden as he'll probably get. "It may not be very close, either," Gerrod says. "But it's *living* history, not just old things in a room. We got a three-year grant from the government, to learn on the job, and it's almost over. So we're thinking in business terms—" He stops in mid-sentence to ponder a persistent ragged green weed. "Do I remember what this is?" he asks himself.

"In the city, we call it mugwort," a teacher offers. "I've heard it's a good bug repellent. I've heard it will enhance your dreams."

"Put it under your pillow, huh," Gerrod says, filing this bit of knowledge away. "We're just now learning," he says. "We're talking more with our elders. And what we do know about plants, you'd have to multiply it by fifteen and *then* we'd have something. Now, clover," he continues, "it has a kind of sweet taste to it. You could make it into a salad or a tea, I think there might be vitamin C in it. Or curly dock. You can use the young leaves for salad, too. Or roast it in a pan, grind it into flour, and make a kind of survival cake with some water and maybe an egg."

Boiled pokeweed, he says, tastes like asparagus, but only if you boil it twice. Chicory smells wonderful but makes lousy coffee. And he's still collecting uses for mullein.

"You can make it into an emergency torch by drying out the spike and coating it with any kind of fat you have around," he says. "Bacon grease or whatever."

"It's also known as camper's toilet paper," one of the teenagers says.

"Yeah, isn't that amazing," Gerrod says. "When it came to things like sanitary uses, you thought in detail, you had the time. Those were different days. Think about way back when there was no TV and no cars and you couldn't buy things. What did you do?"

Silence falls over the group.

"Maybe," Gerrod concludes, "there were things lacking then, but maybe there are things lacking now, too. We used to grow our food. We used to farm drift whales out by the bay. Sometimes," he says, quietly enough to be talking only to himself, "I think it was paradise."

Maybe this is a naive view, he concedes, as we begin to walk back to our cars, but he wants Shinnecock children to have a taste of it anyway.

"This summer, they learned to canoe, they fished, they camped out in the bush, all of it," he says. "I think we made it fun for them. I hope so. See, we're the last that's left. If we don't bring our culture back, it will fizzle. We have to get it back."

We pass a relatively grand house, with new double-paned windows, a landscaped yard, and a big attached garage. In front of it, two young men are shooting hoops, their radio cranking.

"Now, it's those influences," Gerrod says. "I mean, that type of entertainment. I don't want it to take hold." The two boys wave. Gerrod waves back, but does not smile.

Growing up on Shinnecock in the 1960s, Gerrod didn't think about the old ways, either. He doesn't even remember being aware of a time before European immigrants came to Long Island. "I was taught *not* to think about it, actually," he recalls. "First of all, for a long time there was a sense that it wasn't such a proud thing to be native. I thought of myself as a low-level person, and there certainly was never any talk of how our land was lost. That was something I had to reconstruct for myself."

He didn't even attempt it until eight years ago. Before that, he says, he was in a "strictly business frame of mind," earning two community college degrees and running a successful lawn and landscaping business. "I reached a point where, in order to be successful, I had to hire more people and be that big boss guy," he recounts, "so I sold that business, and from that point on, I was a gardener, with hand tools only."

These were skills he'd learned from his father, a lifelong greenskeeper at the Shinnecock Hills Golf Course. "My father grew regular garden vegetables," Gerrod recalls, "and he always wished he could do it full scale. He didn't want to cut grass all his life."

Working less hours for less money, Gerrod had time to think about Shinnecock history—what remained of it, anyway. "We barely have our language anymore," he says. "We were punished for speaking it and we lost it. The reason I travel to the tribes up north, to the other Algonquins, is that they still have their words. Maybe we can get some back."

Even the word *Shinnecock* remains a mystery. On the reservation, I was told it meant "people by the level land" or "people of the meadow."

In Quebec, Gerrod was told it meant "people by the stony shores," and decided he would accept that. (It makes sense—the shores of Shinnecock Bay are still lined with smooth stones.)

During the next eight years, Gerrod looked as far away as Warm Springs, Oregon, for pieces of Indian lore to appropriate. He wasn't picky. American Indian Movement members overhauled his spirituality. Sioux donated a sweat lodge to Shinnecock, and showed them how to use it. "I know the sweat is part of Algonquin history, part of Long Island," Gerrod says, "but again, so many things have been lost."

When we get back to the tribal office, the Parks Department people go home, and I sit in the outer of two small offices waiting for Gerrod's brother, Lamont, who, like many Shinnecock, doesn't have a phone, but has been known to drop by. Lamont, Gerrod says, is the only gardening source the Shinnecock have. He's been growing his own food, relying solely on rainfall for water, for twenty years.

I wait for Lamont all afternoon, surrounded by Shinnecock children. Gerrod's oldest daughter, Aiyana, about to leave for her first year of college, sits at a desk sewing dark purple beads on the ankle cuffs of her powwow regalia. Her friend Rachel Valdez, also on hand to answer one of two phones that seldom rings, is sewing a little and gossiping plenty. Now, when I wander outside, I see the people who were missing before, and they are all children, riding bikes, playing in the dirt, walking down the road with fishing poles. At the end of the afternoon, Gerrod's wife, Josephine, comes by with their youngest child, an eighteen-month-old girl, who runs over to me, climbs into my lap, and plays with my necklace. I can tell she's been raised in a place where it is considered rude to yank at a person's beads.

⟡ ☀ ⟡

Two days later I go back to Shinnecock, still looking for Lamont Smith. Instead, I find Donna Collins, whose title is Collections Manager, but who would rather work in the garden. She seemed the logical choice to take over the work Lamont started. I go out to the garden to meet her and find her standing in a time-honored gardening pose, both hands on her hips, surveying the land—either thrilled or daunted at the prospect of tending it all. She is slim and strong—healthy in the way of a person who spends more time out than in. She is thirty-six. Her black, kinky hair is skinned back into a bun and she looks like the combination of black and Indian she is. At her feet are a bowl made from a dry

141

gourd and the day's crop of thirty zucchini and yellow summer squash.

"I pick every day to keep up with all this," she tells me. "All I wanted was to find out if the soil was capable of producing plants. I guess it is."

She shows me through her inventory of ancient plants, explaining that before this garden was started last year, this plot had been leased to white farmers for more years than anyone could imagine. The corn is an old Iroquois blue variety; interspersed with it are cranberry beans and squash. I was right about the amaranth—except that Donna calls it *calaloo*. She shoos the birds away from *Hadenda tuberosa*, a sort of Indian sunflower with edible tuberous roots.

"Over here are tomatillos, or you can call them ground cherries," Donna says. "And these are the gourds I grow to turn into bowls for soaking seed. It worked last year, even when I forgot and left my seeds soaking for a week instead of overnight."

From the slim literature on Shinnecock anthropology, Donna learned that her people used to dry squash for the winter and store it in cellar holes. The end product tasted "awful," she says, "but it was a taste of a lifestyle I wanted. I wanted to pray to Mother Earth, feed my family, teach them another technique of survival. It was a walk back for me to when life was simpler. I don't know why," she says, "but when my hands are dirty and my back is hurting, it does something for my soul. I love to get out into it."

Last year, it became part of her job to convince a handful of Shinnecock teens to do the same. Otherwise, she says, she could not have kept up with the weeds.

"At first, they all said gardening was too hot, that it was boring," she recalls, "but when I made soup at the end of last year, they became very enthusiastic."

She began in the early morning, starting a friction fire on the site of the Shinnecock village, suspending a dried gourd bowl above the fire, throwing in a slab of bacon, and adding everything the garden offered. "Yellow squash, tomatillos, beans, and peppers," she recalls. "And it cooked all day until it was a wonderful, stewy soup. We all sat outside under the stars and ate it, and it made us all feel real, real good."

Donna says she always felt a heightened sense of *good* on Shinnecock, but as a child she spent much more time outside the reservation than in. Her mother, who was single, often had to leave to find work as a registered nurse. "But we always came here for summers," Donna remembers. "Especially for the powwow." For the first decade after finishing college, Donna worked as a secretary, "because I liked those secretary clothes," she admits, and lived in other states. She always came home for powwow weekends, sometimes from as far away as Miami or St. Croix. But in 1989, pregnant with the first of two daughters, she came back to Shinnecock to stay. "I wanted the support and security," she recalls. "I had a love for Shinnecock within me, because it's a great big place with family security in it. I turned away from the rest of the world, from nine to five, from that feeling of having to keep my head above water."

The secretary clothes she once loved have long been put away. Today she wears baggy shorts, sneakers, and a T-shirt. At the end of the afternoon, we sit in the tribal building's big kitchen, drinking Kool-Aid and eating homemade succotash. It is nothing like the greenish, glutinous stuff from a can that I hated as a child.

"You put in green and red beans, corn, squash, and a bit of brown sugar," Donna says. "It changes character, based on what's fresh in the garden. Some put salt pork in it, but I like it just the way it is."

It's a delicate, sweet soup, and eventually I eat three bowls full. While I do this, I watch a steady stream of women coming in and out, all of whom Donna addresses as Sister or Cousin. Technically, some of them aren't related to her at all. It seems to be based on unadulterated affection. I sit there, eating succotash, for a long time.

ᘓ ☼ ᘔ

I spend the next day researching the Shinnecock past in local libraries, and come to understand why Gerrod Smith—and every other Shinnecock over thirty I spoke to—grew up thinking of himself as a "low-level person."

There have always been gardeners at Shinnecock. In 1627, an observer described the "Souwenox" as the most powerful of Long Island's thirteen tribes, and wrote of their land as a place "where many savages dwell who support themselves by planting maize." Almost immediately after that account, stories of the death of the last "pure-blooded" Shinnecock began to appear. (As recently as the mid-1950s, a real estate company sued the tribe, alleging they had no right to their land because they really weren't Indians anymore.) Local editorials came out against the mixing of black and Shinnecock blood. One writer postulated that half-breeds, like mules, were essentially sterile, and could not reproduce.

Lois Marie Hunter, the Shinnecock author of *The Shinnecock Indians* (1952), spends most of her book praising the selfless ministers of the reservation's Little White Church and their good works.

"The Indian women," Hunter writes, "were excellent natural nurses and cooks . . . they were the only answer to the problem of household help." Perhaps this is why they were "not interested in farming as a livelihood." But even Lois Marie Hunter cannot deny that the Shinnecock knew their plants. In a brief segment on native herb doctor Levi Phillips, she imparts one or two snippets—that an effective eyewash can be made from plantain leaves, that sweet fern can cure dysentery. (Gerrod still uses its crushed leaves to keep mosquitoes away.) But she seems to feel more comfortable writing about how Christianity saved her forebears from a depravity that set in early. In 1741, she writes, the Reverend Asaria Horton found her people to be "an unfortunate group of pagans, seriously and basely addicted to the use of strong drink."

"Yeah, but where'd we *get* that strong drink?" asks Donna Collins, when I quote the passage. "I've been to church. I've done all that. I don't want any more of it."

"Ah well, Lois Marie Hunter," says Elizabeth Haile. "She's one of our most respected elders, but she doesn't have that modern stroke of pride. I just hope we don't lose it."

"What about gardening coming back to the reservation?" I ask. "Won't that help?"

She laughs. "Gardening is not *coming back*, as you put it. We have always grown food. Where else would we have gotten it? When I was a child, if you had money, you saved it to buy shoes with. You traded your corn for my beans, and back and forth. Of course we had gardens. You may not have seen them," she says, "but they were there."

☙ ☀ ❧

Months after I leave Shinnecock, long after their corn and beans have been dried for succotash, long after the ground has frozen, I drive out onto the Plains looking for Indians whose ancestors grew *nothing*. Back East, where I come from, Thanksgiving has the local angle involving pilgrims saved from starvation by maize-growing Indians not unlike the Shinnecock. It's different in the West.

"In the West," Gerrod Smith pointed out, "all the sad stuff that happened, happened a lot more recently. If you want to know the story of all of us, you go out West. They still remember."

What they remember on the Pine Ridge Reservation, which occupies four huge counties in the southwest corner of South Dakota, are the Boss Farm years, during which the Oglala Sioux were supervised by government-appointed white farmers. According to the Sioux Treaty of 1868, the Boss Farmers were charged with turning the Lakota—the name refers loosely to the western third of the South Dakota Sioux—into self-sufficient farmers. It was supposed to take three or four years, at most. But the Boss Farms lasted—inefficiently and uneconomically—into the late 1930s. Denver Indian contacts tell me that older people in Pine Ridge remember the Boss Farm days, and that they don't miss them.

"There never are a lot of great memories associated with a colonial regime," says Greg Gagnon, Vice President of Academic Affairs at Oglala Sioux College. "The Boss Farms came about during our supposed transition to supposedly civilized behavior. But you can't farm here. The soil is terrible, the weather is ugly—I mean, half the *white* farmers failed. And there's no tradition here for farming."

That doesn't mean agriculture never existed among western tribes. Indians along the Missouri River grew corn, beans, and squash—Greg Gagnon calls them "the Big Three." And before moving to South Dakota from Minnesota around the year 1700, Lakota survival depended equally on gardening, hunting and gathering, and fur trapping. But it was the massive buffalo herds that drew them west in the first place—and by the time whites began invading their land, they were almost entirely nomadic. "The Lakota were just not an agricultural people," Greg Gagnon says.

As early as 1893, the Office of Indian Affairs agent at the nearby Rosebud Reservation had the same opinion—not just of the Lakota, but of their allotted land. "This reservation is not adapted to agriculture, as has been practically demonstrated by both Indians and whites," he wrote in his annual report. This did not mean, however, that farming should be abandoned—it seems to have been better than allowing the Indians to remain *uncivilized*. "Indians capable of working," the agent continued, "are required to do some farming and not permitted to spend their entire time in idleness, which invariably breeds discontent and mischief."

Because the Boss Farmers were considered responsible for the Lakota, they kept detailed records of personal lives—including reports on how efficiently each Indian appeared to be striving toward assimilation. If an Indian chose to go in the opposite direction—*away* from progress—the Boss Farmers were authorized to withhold food and money. Particularly discouraged was the ingrained Lakota habit of "roaming."

So Lakota who decided to toe the line had to make an attempt at farming, no matter how hopeless—and it often was. Writer George Hyde, who chronicled western Indian life and history from the turn of the century to the 1930s, remembered Pine Ridge farming this way:

> The Indian women planted their little gardens and went
> through the process which was to become so familiar to them in
> later years. They cared for their little patches, watching them
> eagerly as the young plants grew, and then in mid-September
> saw all their hopes swept away by drought and grasshoppers.

Through relentless phoning, I hear of a man named Joel Swift Bird who is old enough to remember the Boss Farm days, and has even been known to talk into a tape recorder. But when I reach him at the offices of the Foster Grandparent Program, he tells me, through an interpreter, that he has turned off both his hearing aids, and does not wish to turn them on or talk about his life unless I pay him a "copyright licensing fee" of five thousand dollars.

I try to assuage my pride by telling this story to my other Pine Ridge phone contacts, but they think it's very funny.

"I guess we're learning, huh," says Leland Bare Hills, a vocational education instructor at Oglala Sioux College. At fifty-three, he's too young to remember the Boss Farm era, "but when I was a little kid," he recalls, "we grew vegetables every summer, and we did the canning and preserving, too."

This was not uncommon back then, Leland says. While South Dakota soil may have been nearly impossible to farm on a large scale, individual families could often raise enough to eat. "That ended with Lyndon Johnson and the Great Society. It made us more dependent. That was not the intent, but that's what came out of it. Food stamps totally wrecked us. Convenience stores ruined the nutritional life of our people. There's an awful lot of diabetes around here."

Convinced that better nutrition might help alleviate diabetes and other chronic health problems, Leland made a two-acre organic garden part of his vocational educational program nearly twelve years ago. For the past three summers, his Lakota pupils have shared the garden space with exchange students from Bonn, West Germany.

"The fun part is the mixing of culture," he says, "and I like harvesting all the crops by hand." Which is more than he can say for his students, who, after more than a decade of gardening, still prefer building houses to digging dirt. "It's a struggle," Leland admits, "but when you're educating people, it always is."

I love the Colorado plains, the Nebraska hills, and, now, the Badlands, because they remind me of the ocean. But I hate them for being so empty. Driving gradually up and gradually down, my five-year-old daughter chattering away in the passenger seat, there is nothing to think about but yucca, grass, tumbleweeds, and emptiness.

Crossing onto Pine Ridge is no gentle transition. After hundreds of miles of prosperous ranches and white clapboard towns along the railroad tracks, we're suddenly in a foreign land where people seem very poor and very desperate. Spent cars and beer bottles litter the ditches. The looks we get are neither friendly nor curious. Inside the tribal administration building we meet Sandy, who draws us a map to the home of Bernard Little White Man, known around the county as a dedicated gardener.

"If you don't find his house, go here," Sandy says, placing an X on the map. "My mother lives there. Go in and say hello to her."

We set off down dirt roads, quickly losing the trail of Sandy's mother and everyone else on the map. After several hours, we hit a dead-end road with the usual two houses on a rise above it—an old frame structure with broken windows and a government house set onto a cement pad. An inside-out truck tire holds what remains of a clump of marigolds. We are standing there, looking confused, when an old woman in a short-sleeved housedress and apron comes out into the freezing wind and smiles.

"Who are you?" she asks.

She doesn't laugh at us for searching out gardens in November. "My husband and I always had one," she says. "We grew tomatoes, carrots, potatoes, corn, and peas. But he's been gone fourteen years now, and since then, I'd rather sew quilts. My name is Emily Has No Horse. I was born seventy-five years ago in that other house," she adds, knowing I am trying to guess her age, since she looks youthful and toothless at the same time.

"Do you remember Boss Farms?" I ask.

"Yes," she says, "but nobody forces us to do nothin' these days. They used to be hard on us, but now they're not allowed to be. We're not savages no more, you see?"

There is a beat, during which I realize this is a joke. Then all three of us laugh, especially my daughter.

It turns out Bernard Little White Man lives just over the hill, and we set out to walk there. "Next time," Emily Has No Horse calls after us, "come and stay longer than you planned!"

His son tells us Bernard Little White Man is back in the tall grass, working on an old wooden house. We take a single track trail to get there. When we find him, Bernard is wearing quilted coveralls and a hat with earflaps. His face is wrinkled and leathery from sun. He leads us into his modern house, which is covered with Christian sayings on plaques, and tells us about working the earth in the tough South Dakota weather.

"We have just three months to make a crop," he says, "and then, we don't know—a frost or a blizzard can come any time. Just about all my life I've tried growing things. Tomatoes, canning vegetables. But you know," he adds, "my wife died two years ago, and since then, I just don't. We used to work the garden together."

"Do you remember the Boss Farms?" I ask.

He does, but he won't talk about them.

On the way back down the dirt road to the town of Pine Ridge, my daughter spots something neither of us had noticed before. Far from the road, on a hillside covered with blond, frost-trimmed grass, there is a huge pole thrust into the earth, flying a wildly colored flag. In a half-circle around it, covering a territory of perhaps three hundred yards, there is a series of wooden poles and cross-beams. We can just make out the figure of a man with long black braids down his back walking purposefully across the grass.

Later, at a gas station, I describe the place to the teenage boy behind the counter. He tells me they are the Sun Dance grounds.

We drive back to look at them some more. I tell my daughter the little I know—that Sun Dancers go for days without food or water, doing a kind of shuffling step and hoping to see visions, and that they have done this for hundreds of years. I get stuck trying to explain the word "vision," though, and we fall into an agreeable silence.

The man with the braids has gone, and no one is dancing, but the flag is whipping in the air. The wooden poles seem immovable as Stonehenge. They are planted in this ground.

9 Road Trip: Medicine

What is it about gardening
that works out something bad?

ANNE CHOTZINOFF GROSSMAN

When I first saw Lillian McCracken, she was minding a stand at the Colorado Organic Growers' farm fair. On a small table before her were buckets of giant dried blue larkspur and an assortment of homemade remedies. In a long blue skirt, with her dark blond hair down her back, Lillian looked like some kind of impossibly healthy pioneer woman.

"People respond to my appearance of vitality," she said evenly. "I'm fifty years old, but I look younger."

She looked much younger. Her face was tan, round, smooth, and slathered with a kind of glowing grease called Calendula Creme. I bought a jar. Lillian told me she cooks it up in her spare bedroom in a farmhouse in Saguache, a tiny town three hours south of Denver. It looked like a small tub of vaseline and smelled, not unpleasantly, of marigold pollen. It cost me four dollars. I smoothed it on my face. It made me look greasy, but well preserved. I read the list of ingredients—mugwort, olive oil, comfrey root, and something called vegetable gelly.

"What else do you make in that spare bedroom?" I asked Lillian.

"Lots," she said.

This was a complete understatement. I looked Lillian up in the state organic growers' guide and learned that she and her husband, Thomas, produce not just cosmetics and herbal cures, but vegetables, herbs, flowers, and quinoa, the Andean grain no health food store would catch themselves dead without. They call their place Green Earth Farms.

It seemed a reasonable beginning to my trip—especially since I had no idea where I was going, only that I would be gone about two weeks and hoped to meet people who cultivated the earth. At least I'd seen Lillian once, and liked the sight of her. She also had a slightly bossy manner, as if she had answers and would not hesitate to impart them. People without firm travel plans gravitate to that sort of thing.

When I get to Green Earth Farms, it is devoid of McCrackens. Their kitchen door swings open. I yell. No one answers. Around the hundred-year-old farmhouse are old cottonwoods. As I stand there, an enormous tom turkey and an old dog that looks like a stuffed sheep attach themselves to me. The three of us walk down to the vegetable garden. With the dog and the turkey right behind, I trudge through three acres of organic vegetables—all cole crops and as healthy as Lillian herself, especially the cabbages, which, with their outer leaves, have three-foot wingspans. On the edges of the field are drifts of larkspur. The land is high, about eight thousand feet, and the colors are clear and intense. When the clouds pass away from the sun, I am almost warm enough to relax. What I am doing instead is considering my station wagon, which is not empty.

In the passenger seat, in the shade, twenty-year-old Sonjia Clark sits reading *Cosmo*. I have no idea how she will work out as a traveling companion. We are fifteen years apart in age and worlds apart in orientation. Since leaving home yesterday, we have not discussed the fact that Sonjia would rather be finishing her first year of college than driving toward the Gulf of Mexico with me. Her mother, who has been daycare provider for three of my daughter's four years, would prefer this option, too. But seven months ago, over Christmas vacation, Sonjia was diagnosed with lupus. Since then, she's been living at home, having gained thirty pounds and a moon face from steroid therapy. Her fingernails sometimes turn black from poor circulation. Sometimes, for some reason, there are midnight visits to the emergency room. But Sonjia always says she's feeling fine. I suspect she hopes to wake up some morning soon and find the lupus gone, her independence (and her social life) restored. But all I really know is that she came on this trip because she was bored.

Well, and because there is nothing I hate as much as being alone for a long time, over a long distance, in a car. Oddly, this very experience is one I have sought out repeatedly, ever since I got a driver's license. Filling my car with gas for this particular trip, I felt panic. I drove home to load the last few camping supplies—the mildewed Boy Scout tent, the underpowered white gas stove—and decided it would be better not to feel it, think about it, talk about it. Instead, I would show Sonjia—who does not know the geography of the United States—the world.

So here we are. We do not yet know we are on the trail of bush doctors.

We are still in the middle of introductions when I begin to wonder if Lillian McCracken is some kind of witch. We are standing in her living room, which is littered with clothes, a futon, an incongruously fancy TV and VCR, and dried flower bouquets hanging from the rafters. Sonjia, who has looked pale since morning, falls into a chair.

"How *are* you?" Lillian asks sternly, though they have just met.

"I have a headache," Sonjia says, in a little voice.

"Oh. Okay, then," Lillian says. I follow her into the kitchen, also littered, but with dishes, brown bottles of homemade tonics, more dried flowers. In a matter of seconds, she mixes together a glass of her own homemade headache remedy. She brings it out to Sonjia, who looks slightly alarmed.

"How is it?" I ask, after she drains the cup.

"Like nothing I ever tasted before," she says.

"What's in it?" I ask Lillian.

"Wormwood, meadowsweet, wild yarrow, rosemary, feverfew."

"You grow all that?"

"Yeah." Next, Lillian grabs a spray bottle filled with orange flower water and lavender, mists the air around Sonjia's face with it, and disperses it with a feather. "Tomorrow's the exact Uranus/Neptune connection. Yesterday I couldn't do a thing. *You,*" she tells Sonjia, "are probably being strongly affected."

Either because this is the weirdest treatment Sonjia has received yet, or because she is worn out, she lies back on the comfy chair and closes her eyes.

"Okay, then," Lillian says, turning to me.

I follow her out into the countryside, unable to take my eyes off her feet. They are incredibly strong, gnarled, dirt-encrusted—more like hooves or claws, and yet beautiful. They are proud, fortified feet, flapping along in sandals. She exudes a sort of pure hippiness. Pure gardening, too.

"On my father's side, my family were Italian farmers who moved to the Bay Area," she tells me. "That's where I grew up. I remember my grandfather's artichoke patch. My grandmother had a little one-acre farm, right where San Francisco and Daly City meet. She gave us herbs when we were sick, chamomile and that sort of thing, and everything we ate had rosemary and thyme in it."

In the early sixties, Lillian worked at the University of San Francisco anthropology department—and, like others there, immersed herself in the anti–Vietnam War movement. "I was at the first love-in and the first be-in," she recalls, "but my path was always yoga and meditation. I'd try a drug and think, that's okay, but it's not as good as yoga and meditation."

By 1975, totally steeped in eastern religion, Lillian went with her husband and two small children (ages seven and eight) to Nepal. "My husband took off for the most remote monastery," she recalls. "He was the first westerner to ever see it, and he underwent purification for the upper three chakras there. My children and I couldn't go—my son had hepatitis. Well, my husband decided to come back for my daughter's ninth birthday, so he hiked for fifteen miles in a blizzard and when he got back, he went into a coma for twelve days."

"And then what happened?" I ask.

Lillian shoves the tom turkey aside. "Have you ever noticed how stupid turkeys are?" she asks. "They're so stupid they'll hold their breath and literally turn blue before they remember to breathe again."

I watch the turkey. What Lillian says is true. "But what about your husband?" I ask.

"He died," Lillian says, meeting my eye. "But it was a luminous experience, an altered state. Every day he got more beautiful. It was a very elevated death—a transition instead of something awful. He came back into his body at the end, he knew he was going to die, and I said, 'Should we go back home?' and he said no. At the hospital, the women would grieve and ululate. I felt free to do that, too, and no one blinked. So he died."

She stayed in Nepal that Christmas season. Her two children found friends to play with and Lillian did some deliberate grieving. They moved on—traveling through Sri Lanka for six months—and returned to northern California in late 1976, where Lillian immediately took up gardening. Soon after that, she met a man.

"He was what they call a nature cure doctor," she says. "His emphasis was that food is medicine." Years of extreme eating—what she calls nutrification and purification—followed. Today, she says, her theory is much simpler: "Whatever your heritage is, you should eat from the peasant diet of that culture."

Whatever she ate, though, was organic and home grown. In the next ten years, Lillian and her children lived on a series of agricultural communes, including the tree planting collective where she met Thomas. She planted trees with him for three years—"I have no disdain for manual labor"—and then, in 1986, they came up to Saguache, where they bought 240 acres bordered by the Sangre de Cristo Mountains and bisected by a stream. Nine years later, their produce is the darling of all the hippest Colorado health food supermarkets.

"It may seem like a small town to you," Lillian says. "But, I can work twenty-four hours a day if I want to. I grow the vegetables, herbs, and flowers, I'm an astrological counselor, and I do herbal research and formulas. One of the few things the Bible says that I believe is from dust we came and to dust we shall return. If you don't work the earth, you lose your ability to sustain the harmony of the physical body. And people want to have that appearance of harmony and vitality. You can't have that if you don't work outside, in the earth."

I follow her prodigious feet into a new greenhouse—south facing, its north wall buried in the dirt, with speakers to play music to the plants. "We were hoping to grow year-round, but it's more like June through October," Lillian says. "March and April are all herbs."

Purple basil alone has made the construction of the greenhouse worthwhile, and yuppie greens (radicchio, fennel, gourmet lettuce) are a fine cash crop at four dollars per pound, wholesale. I find plum tomatoes and cucumber vines still producing. I get a bag of groceries, plus several eggs fresh from the hen. Lillian is happy to give them to me, because, she says, "Food is a transforming of elemental energy." Then she spends five minutes—none of which I understand—berating the World Bank. When the air clears, I'm standing in the kitchen next to Thomas, a tall, thin man in overalls with long, curly blond hair down his back. He looks even younger than Lillian. He asks if I'd like an elk burger.

"I could have sworn you'd both be vegetarians," I say.

"Well, we're not," Lillian says. "There's no system."

In the living room, Sonjia is reading a book on Colorado weeds. "I feel better," she says. "In fact, I felt better almost right away. It was weird. Don't you like these dried flowers? These people are cool. Her husband offered me an elk burger. I might tell her about my lupus," Sonjia decides.

First, Lillian wants to see Sonjia's traveling pharmacy—the four different medications she takes to keep her symptoms away. "Do you *want* to take all this?" she asks Sonjia.

"No," Sonjia says, a little uncertainly. "Well, the prednisone. It's a steroid. I hate that."

Lillian invites us to convoy twenty miles east to the small, counter-culture town of Crestone so that Sonjia can talk to a woman named Faye. Though its population holds steady at under a thousand people, Crestone is crawling with astrologers, holistic health practitioners, and old hippies. Faye, I think, will be one of the three. "Faye has lupus, too," Lillian tells Sonjia. "But she's off steroids. Maybe she can help."

Inside Faye's tiny consulting room, Sonjia is hoisted onto a massage table. Without taking Sonjia's clothes off, Faye touches her thoroughly, as if she were a mother baboon picking nits off a baby. She asks Sonjia about her symptoms, discusses herbal cures, and tosses around certain remedies I consider ridiculous—cold foods only, or going off steroids altogether. I look at my watch, then at Sonjia, who is crying quietly.

"It felt good to tell them," she explains later. "I thought they understood."

That night, she builds a fire and begins brewing a tea from the dendrilion and licorice roots Lillian has sold her. The next morning, she knocks down the first of many daily pills with a cup of this dark, smelly tea.

A thousand miles go by, leaving us plenty of time to talk. Sonjia tells me her boyfriend history. I show her my road atlas, explaining, as if to a child, that we are headed *southeast*. Some nights, we split a six-pack of Corona, after which it no longer seems ridiculous to read each other's poetry aloud. We talk about sex, drugs, rock and roll—and even gardening. Since Lillian, I've been thinking about bush doctors.

I first heard the term on the British Virgin Island of Tortola, from a cab driver named Ritsel Lettsome.

"Grow things, make medicine, find roots. Better than a real doctor," he said. I never saw Ritsel again, but ever since then I have had a lingering interest. I like the idea of gardeners who cure. I like the chutzpah of it—bush doctors in the late twentieth century. They aren't supposed to exist, but they do.

"What is lupus, exactly?" I ask Sonjia, as we drive toward Port Arthur, Texas.

"I don't know, really," she says. "I have this book about it, but I haven't read it yet."

That night, at a campground on the Gulf of Mexico, a ranger offers us a forty-mile strip of beach to camp on. "Y'all just drive your car out there and pick wherever. And better get you something for the mosquitoes," he says. "It's fixin' to rain about a foot tonight."

We don't see a cloud anywhere, but just after midnight, the rain starts. Every mosquito for forty miles around rushes into our tent to get out of it. The night becomes too hot and too cold at the same time. We don't sleep, either—you can't swat a mosquito and sleep simultaneously. At dawn, we stop trying.

Two hours later, we cross into Louisiana, still in the rain. Sonjia is sleeping, her face more gray than white, except for the red mosquito bites. In Lafayette, I splurge on a motel room. Once inside it, Sonjia collapses on her bed and turns on the TV. In one hand is her unread lupus book. In the other is a glass of herb tea.

"Are you okay?" I ask. She says she's fine.

❦ ☀ ❦

Louisiana, as far as I can tell, isn't really a part of America at all. I hear Cajun French on the airwaves instead of standardized Country Crap. Food, especially cheap food, is so good, in its individually seasoned way, that few franchises dare to penetrate. There are no bad cups of coffee anywhere in the state. Also, there is wildness in the air. I remember reading that the Louisiana murder rate was unnaturally high. A bush doctor would thrive in a place like this. The Chamber of Commerce people suggest I call in at an herb store five miles out in the country, down a road with the charming name of Pinhook.

When I get there, I meet a slight, dark-haired woman with black eyes. She is wearing a wildflower sweatshirt and twining an elaborate dried-flower wreath. Above her, grapevines snake in sine curves across the ceiling.

"What you're looking for is what we call a *traiteur*," she says, pronouncing the "r"s with a roll that sounds more Italian than French. "Around here, it's common. When my little brother was very young, he had warts and my father took him out to a *traiteur* at Bayou Chicot and he said a few things and gave him a few herbs and the warts disappeared. It seemed to be a spiritual thing, as well as the use of folk plants."

"Do you believe in *traiteurs*?" I ask.

"Some of these things, it's a fine line whether it'll heal you or kill you," she says. "But I take an interest in it, because my thing is herbs. I been growing them since 1975. I found this book in the library about growing herbs in containers and I used to mail away for seeds."

"Couldn't you just go to the store?" I ask.

"No," she says. "You want some coffee?"

I do. I let my unspoken *why* hang in the air.

"I was in the federal women's penitentiary at the time," the woman continues. "For armed robbery. I was a junkie."

I look around the shop, with its stenciled walls, dried flowers, potpourri bags, and hand-lettered jars of jam.

"What's your name?" I ask.

"Lydia D'Aigle Fontenot," she says. "I was born in Ville Platte, just up the road."

Just up the road, where *traiteurs* cure warts and the damp fall weather is sometimes broken up by a warm, dry Christmas Day you can celebrate in your shirtsleeves, Lydia's parents had a big kitchen garden for canning and eating. "They made me weed it," she says. "But it was a punishment to me."

It was only in a federal women's prison in Virginia that she began to care for growing things. "I learned that it's an innate need, gardening," she recalls. "How could you not? If you plant something and it produces fruit and you are experiencing the plant fully, how could you not? I'm saying, I've lived the other way and I wouldn't trade what I have now."

Lydia spent the first few months after prison in a rustic house on a bayou owned by family friends. "I stayed there picking blackberries, fishing, and swimming," Lydia remembers, "and their son Bill was there some, too. Neither of us were looking for a relationship."

Bill and Lydia Fontenot were married two years later, bought a wino crash pad for three thousand dollars, and moved it onto a piece of low land with a bayou running past it. Lydia became the executive director of a shelter for homeless women and children, and Bill went to work in the oil field, "which, if he hadn't," Lydia says, "we couldn't live the way we do—simply, but well."

In 1984, Bill got his Ph.D. in ecology and took over the natural history museum in Lafayette. Burned out on human misery, Lydia gave up social service and began making crafts from herbs and dried flowers. Bill developed a passion for native plants, and started taking on side jobs as a landscape designer.

"And he collects plants and information about plants," she says. "I think he might know a *traiteur*. You want me to call him?"

She finds him, lucky for me, in the middle of a rare day off. "But you better hurry," she says, "he may feel like taking off, and if he does, he will."

I jump in the car and drive back through Lafayette as fast as I can. I am in a completely overexcited state—imagine being this close to a *traiteur* this fast, not to mention herbs and armed robbery. Oblivious to a changing light, I rear-end an elaborately coiffed black woman's late-model Mercury. There is a crunching sound. Suddenly, at least one person appears on each of twenty wooden porches on the street. Everyone begins to talk excitedly. The smashed woman exits her car, walks up to me, and says, in a thick French accent: "Honey, honey, what you do to my husband's *car?*"

"I don't know," I answer.

"Well, honey there ain't a nick on it," the woman decides. "So, you okay?"

"Yeah, why she so *noivous?*" asks one of the porch-sitters, who has come out into the street for a better look. "What you need," he tells me, "is to go get you a shot of whiskey somewhere."

"That's right," says my victim, nodding her head emphatically.

"Don't you want my insurance stuff?" I ask.

"*Hell* no," she says. Then she hops in her car and speeds away, leaving me standing there *noivous*, but exhilarated at having been in a genuine Cajun car crash.

Bill Fontenot turns out to be a large, handsome, bearded man who shares my enthusiasm for cheap comfort food. He hands me some coffee, and sits me in front of a fireplace. "No cream?" he says. "Where's your Cajun, anyway?"

"Okay," I say, "bring on the cream."

Before getting anywhere near the subject of *traiteurs* and native plants, we plan two eating outings—one to a blue-plate special diner and one to a well-known Cajun place "where they got music," Bill says, "and the food! Well, some boy from Montana cooks there, but he's beautiful, all the Cajuns love him."

That established, he tells me about the *traiteur*. "I never actually call him that to his face," Bill says. "It's not a word you wanna use around them. I mean, if *he* says it first . . . ."

"How did you meet him?" I ask.

"About four years ago, at the native crafts festival, he came up to the booth where I was selling plants. He brought me a plant. He said, 'Do you know what *this* is?' And I said, 'No,' and he said, 'Well, it's the first one you *better* know 'cause it breaks a fever.' And I fully believe it does. He turns out to be right more often than not, and I'm happier and happier to see him. I don't know his name or anything. I'm not sure I'd ask, either."

"Why not?"

"Well, with Indians, they don't always tell you what they know, and with Cajuns it's faith healing as much as plant healing," Bill says. "This old guy is Cajun and Indian at the same time. You got to be sensitive to him. Like he'll never take money for a cure, ever. He doesn't think it's spiritually right."

When I wake up the next morning Sonjia, though flat on her back and lying perfectly motionless, is wide awake. Tears are pouring soundlessly out of her eyes.

"What's wrong?" I ask.

"It hurts," she says. "I need to go to the bathroom, but I can't sit up."

I put my arms around her shoulders and haul her into a sitting position. I swing her legs around to hang from the edge of the bed, then lift her up to stand. I ask if she can walk, and she says she can. But it is an old woman's walk.

Sonjia's lupus has caught up with her. Her joints and lungs ache, her fingertips are black, and she has a temperature of 105. I ply her with Gatorade and pills. When she falls asleep, I skim through the lupus book. What can be done about lupus, especially when it flares, is nothing. But Sonjia insists on her herbs, and I boil them for her.

We check her temperature every half hour throughout the day, and as it inches down, we begin watching terrible TV movies. Why she finally reaches normal and why her fingertips stop being black, we never know. It is a scary, twenty-four-hour day.

By ten-thirty the next morning we are both settled in rocking chairs in front of space heaters in Lydia Fontenot's kitchen, watching her make herb jelly, and listening to her comforting talk of sweet Annie, lemon grass, and rosemary, "which grows around here like a broom. Now remind me," she says, "y'all are each going to take some jelly back with you when you go."

All around us are bundles of everlasting flowers, wreaths, and pomander balls; stacks of books; sacks of various kinds of animal chow to feed everything but the spiders and lizards that run free in this house, "and therefore," Lydia says, "we don't have roaches. I just take the webs down once a year and other than that I don't bother the spiders."

Lydia is a sucker for animals. Outside, in cages, are fifteen different orphans—raccoons, beavers, muskrats, birds—rescued from the bayou. "Boy, I *need* to do these craft shows coming up," she says. "All those animals get expensive. Eighty pounds of dogfood and formula a week. It's not a bad life, though. It's a natural extension of growing things, making art out of them."

Her crafts room—just off the kitchen and littered with sprigs of St. John's wort and blue veronica—gives off a clean, strong smell, almost limy. She calls the plant it comes from vedivert. "A real earthy smell. I nearly broke a shovel trying to dig it up," she says. "Take some, it'll sweeten your linens."

Then she puts on her heavy-duty leather gloves, and we go outside to feed the animals.

The Fontenots' two-acre garden is fenced by woods and twenty-foot-high pampas grass. On the woodland side are banks of cages on four-foot stilts—"The bayou'll flood up to five feet, and last year it came right in the house three times," Lydia says. Stretching out before the rescued animals are raised beds planted in tangles of herbs, everlasting flowers, and roses, with Bill's native plants taking over where grass used to be. Three dogs, all old or injured, follow us as we walk around.

"We live in a floodplain," Lydia says, "and when we came in 1982 all there was, was dewberry growing wild, 'cause it was farmland and the earth had been made sterile by all those chemicals. We've watched the land reclaim itself, all the plants take over again. In the summer, I'm gardening right alongside cottonmouths and copperheads. I used to be terrified, but now I use a hoe and put them in a bucket. Gardening's such strange work. But then," she decides, "you sleep well at night."

In the cages, we flirt with a baby raccoon known as Lucky Stars, "because she grabbed aholt of a floating limb and stayed alive" and Pillsbury the beaver—"a sweet creature," Lydia says. "I'm fixin' to put her back in the wild, which is such a rush there's nothing like it. But there's always animals on their way in or on their way out around here. Practically no one knows how to take care of them but me."

"Do you ever leave home, even for a few days?" I ask.

"Not too often," she says.

We say good-bye to Lydia outside a Cajun cafeteria where Bill and I stuff ourselves on boudin, red beans and rice, and something he calls "that mo' betta dessert. You better finish your plate," he warns Sonjia. "If Evelyn sees you not eating, she gon' come over and say: 'What's the matter, baby, you sick? Can I fix you something different?'"

The rest of the afternoon will be typical for Bill and Lydia—she canning herb jellies for a crafts fair tomorrow, he making spaghetti sauce with the parish priest for a fund-raising dinner. The Fontenots pile us up with food—pounds of Louisiana coffee, jellies, herbs to put around our house in bowls, extra boudin in case we should lose our Cajun on the trip home, which we intend to start before dark.

"But first," Bill says, "we gon' try and find that *traiteur*."

I follow behind his truck for twenty minutes, until he pulls over beside a rusty wire fence, beyond which I see a tangle of underbrush and hear the barking of unseen hound dogs.

"He's not here yet," Bill tells us, as we lean on our cars. "We'll wait on him. Don't call him a *traiteur*, remember, don't ask his name, and if he gives you a cure, or a plant or something, don't say thank you. It breaks the spell."

I smell the *traiteur* before I see him—a strange, bitter smell, very pungent, but also somehow antiseptic. He has an old man's face, with long, gray hair covered by a Winston cigarette cap. His body, in overalls and a T-shirt, is muscled, lean, and flexible. Much younger than his face.

Without taking any notice of either me or Sonjia, he jumps into the continuation of the conversation he was having with Bill when they last saw each other three months ago. His voice is raspy, very Cajun, with French words thrown in.

"You know this black cherry plant?" he asks Bill. "It makes a blue passion flower? You pick it, it kinda wilt, and then you break it up and eat it."

"Yeah, I heard of that," Bill says companionably. They help each other through the fence and begin walking through the *traiteur*'s property, which is mostly overgrown weeds and scrub trees. Only the *traiteur* knows where he has planted things on purpose, and which have grown up by accident. Bill stops by a clump of tiny yellow flowers.

"Now that's monglié, right?" he asks.

"That's it," the *traiteur* answers. "They say it will cure a fever. I say no way. But you drink it in the springtime, like a rabbit, it flush out your system, make you ready for the beautiful weather. Now this stuff here, it got seeds what fall all over like cotton."

"I know what you talking about," Bill says, his accent growing more colloquial by the second. "I saw some a this before."

"Well, what I do, I put it in a jug, and I drink some of it whenever I pass that jug by. It's real good. Hell, you can get drunk to fall on the floor, and drink some of this, and be okay an hour later."

"What you call it?"

"*La chasse pâle*," the *traiteur* says. "But you might have an American name for it."

Now the *traiteur*'s house comes into view—an old wooden structure, with no glass in the windows. Around it, in the tall grass, no less than five lawnmowers are stopped in their tracks. About fifty feet off, from inside a corrugated shack, I hear hounds barking and snuffling.

"Your daddy was a Choctaw?" Bill asks him, as he has probably asked many times before.

"Oh, yes. My mama was six foot three, hundred-and-eighty-five pounds. My sisters all were, too. My brothers were huge. I'm not so big, but I'm just sixty-eight years old, so hey. I got my gift handed down from *mon oncle* and my two grammas. We all knew how to do it, but you got to sacrifice something in your life to use it, you see. Hey, you," he says, addressing me for the first time. He takes off down a hill behind his house, motioning me to follow.

In a minute, we're standing on a rickety dock at the banks of a muddy river. "This here, what I wanted to show you, is Bayou Teche," he says. "Eight-foot alligator be swimming down here, his mouth open. Sort of a brownish black."

Involuntarily, I take a few steps back from the shoreline.

"Now this," he continues, grabbing a handful of prehistoric jointed plants that grow half underwater, "this is lizard tail, that's good stuff, y'all. You cut notches, make a little necklace of it, and you won't get sick. Or soak it three days and drink it. Don't you be boiling it, just soak it. You won't get sick. Now that other girl? She already sick."

"Sonjia?" I ask.

"Her," he says. "You want me to treat her?"

"Treat her?" I say.

"I'm a *traiteur*, in other words," he says patiently. "I got people to heal."

"What's your name?" I ask, violating both rules at once.

"Jay Hebert," he says promptly, then dictates his address. "And when you write something down, you send it to me. And put in this: You can paint your face and body with pokeweed, for a rash, like poison ivy or poison oak. But better, much mo' better, is Comet."

"Comet? The cleanser?"

"That the stuff. You make it up into a paste and put it on the rash, and when it starts to draw, it breaks that itch right off."

"What do you do for a headache, Monsieur Hebert?" I ask.

"For a headache," he fires back, "you should walk and not talk until you in a pool of sweat. I treat all hiccups, too—but not the hiccup of death, that no one can treat. I take catalpa leaves, put them on a little baby what's coughing. The leaves just wilt up and the fever will break, save another little baby. Now this," he says, bending down to pick a feathery green weed, "the wild quails love. I call it *viné rare*. You drink this, fever's gonna drop outa you real quick."

For another two hours I follow Bill and Monsieur Hebert as they stroll through the plants, trading knowledge of the botanical world and backwoods medicine. (*This here is sommlier. No, it ain't, it's labachien. That right? That right.*)

As Sonjia and I get ready to leave, the *traiteur* takes me aside: "You want me to treat her?" he asks again. I realize that he thinks I'm Sonjia's mother.

"You need to ask her," I say. Sonjia shrinks from the *traiteur*—maybe from his smell. He doesn't seem to mind. "I got lots of other people to treat," he says. "You know, I can make a snake roll up like a donut, and I can unwind him. I'm *busy*." But he hands me a branch of wax myrtle. "Make her a tea with that," he insists. "And take some of this red buckeye, too. It keeps the evil force away."

"What do I do with it?" I ask.

"Just keep it by you," he says. "That evil force go somewhere else, then, maybe." I think of saying thank you, but who am I to break a spell?

"No way I was going to let him treat me," Sonjia laughs, as we start our two-day drive home. "Comet! I mean, no way." Then she takes her pills, swallowing them down with Lillian's herbal tea. We both agree to keep the red buckeye around, just in case. Real medicine is nice, but only a fool ignores the bush doctor.

Lydia Fontenot's Unusual, Delicious Jelly ❦ to Serve with Chicken or Cheese ❧

Boil four cups of apple juice, and put in leaves of mountain mint, peppermint, or eucalyptus—maybe all three. Steep it till it becomes a tea, about fifteen minutes. Strain it, add cider vinegar, sugar, and fruit pectin. Then, when you put it in jars, add a mint leaf to each.

Jay Hebert's Recipe for ❦ Venison Jerky ❧

Shoot you a deer, cut it up in strips, dry it, and put it on a string. Knock them blue fly eggs off it, and watch it very close. When it be dry you could put something on top of it, like melted tallow. It will keep you going all day long.

10 Road Trip:
Three Days in Oregon

. . . there is not a sprig of grass that shoots
uninteresting to me.

THOMAS JEFFERSON TO HIS DAUGHTER MARTHA
RANDOLPH, DECEMBER 23, 1790

At the end of a long, hot, desiccated Denver, I realize I look and feel like my own garden. Burnt out, dying for moisture. I long to go where I've never been before. I want to spend the daylight hours in other people's gardens, asking questions, smelling new smells, touching new dirt. I want salt water and sea level. As if by heavenly design, I end up in Portland.

Getting my bearings, I walk through a neighborhood not far southeast of downtown Portland. It's been described to me as slummy, but I amend that to *slobby*—one of Aunt Cookie's highest compliments. In this landscape, I'm put completely at ease. Consider the evidence:

Plants grow huge here. Rose hips the size of Ping-Pong balls, hydrangea blooms as big as basketballs. Semi-dwarf fruit trees thirty feet tall. Pampas grass fronds tapping at second-story windows.

The houses ramble—large, wooden, unkempt—with porches, stoops, places to hang out and watch the street or enjoy the yard. Just as perfectly restored, paint-by-numbers Victorians leave me cold, these slightly peeling Queen Annes leave me warm—as if happy, messy families are being raised inside them.

Lawns are ratty, most of them downright dormant. There has been a water shortage this summer and no one seems to care.

Many, many flowers are the color of salmon. Even more of them are blue.

I turn a corner, past a slope of geranium that gives off a licorice smell, and head for the three-story house at the end of the block.

Lucy Hardiman meets me at the door. She is forty-eight, with black hair in a sleek bob, and, except for bright pink lipstick, very casual. She takes me up to the second floor of the house, where a group of men and women in their early twenties are standing around drinking coffee. Her husband, Fred, can just be seen through the second-story window balancing on a ladder with a can of paint. After a while, I determine that none of these people are Fred or Lucy's children.

"Do you *have* kids?" I ask.

"Yes, one," says Lucy. "She lives here, but she's not here now. The rest of these people are our tenants, but we're also sort of a large, extended family."

"Your basic equal opportunity landlords," Fred yells through the window.

When we get down to the street, I see what she's talking about. Next to Lucy and Fred's large old house is a square frame house with four apartments in it. In the fourteen years since Fred and Lucy moved here and bought the apartment building, they have never once advertised for tenants. They just show up—staying, Lucy says, for an average of five years.

"We actually had a philosophical vision," she tells me. "This *was* a slum. We wanted to create affordable housing in the city for middle-income people, and we wanted to give them real amenities, like a garden."

In the beginning, she says, it was a communal garden. The yard, which had been nothing but a fifty-by-one-hundred-foot vacant lot, was turned into a vegetable garden so that Fred and Lucy's intentional community could grow its own food.

It didn't work. "We didn't want to police people is why," Lucy remembers. "So I looked at the garden again and decided I would do what I felt. Perennials, shrubs, trees, textures, and blooms. A lot of what I am is here, as it turns out. And by the way," she says, as we push aside ten-foot-tall rose canes to enter the garden, "you came at completely the wrong time of year. The garden usually looks much, much better."

I can't imagine how. Laid out in geometric beds on three sides of a rectangle of lawn, the garden is a mass of heights, with flowers crammed in everywhere, branches, vines, shrubs all mixed together and hanging over me as I walk down narrow brick-in-sand paths. Six-foot-tall cosmos, overblown roses—some still in bloom, some with huge hips—scramble into the fruit trees. Clematis snakes all over, its feathery seed heads intact. Blue aster, rudbeckia, and Russian sage crowd around a weathered wood trellis with a bench below it. There is green wicker furniture anywhere you might want to sit down and admire the view. On the fourth side of the garden are the two decks attached to Fred and

Lucy's house, both crowded with pots of flowers and Japanese-looking trees.

"*Nothing* was here when you bought this place?"

"Not one tree," Lucy says.

"Wow."

She waits for me to say something more knowledgeable. When I don't, she says: "It's not a cottage garden, you know."

"No?" I always thought of a cottage garden as a series of riotous borders generally located against a cottage or a house. Which this certainly resembles.

"No," Lucy says. "A cottage garden is amorphous. The shapes here are rectilinear. It's actually *very* structured, and within that, this garden can be what it wants to be. Each bed is very mixed—trees, deciduous shrubs, annuals, bulbs—you don't have all that in a cottage garden. And it changes all year long. Even in December, there are berries and barks, and because of the walkways, you see the bones of the garden everywhere."

I never thought of a garden from the skeleton out before. Now I can see why people would hire Lucy to help them redesign their gardens—which is what she will be doing most of today, a Sunday. During the rest of the week, she sells clothing for Norm Thompson, a catalog outlet. At the height of the growing season, late spring and summer, she scales that job back to three days per week. She's also the vice president of Portland's Hardy Plant Society, which is one of the most eccentrically devoted garden clubs in the country. I've talked to several Hardy Plant people on the phone, and not one of them is remotely conversant with the view that gardening—especially garden *club* gardening—is a frivolous pursuit undertaken by the leisure class.

"*What?*" Lucy says, when I expound this theory. "It's not frivolous at all! I would take umbrage to that suggestion! Gardening is a creative act. I can't draw and I can't paint, but I can create something. That's frivolous?"

And another thing, she says: this garden is *used*. Two tenant weddings, decks as outdoor rooms—and even as we talk, I realize that not just one well-mannered Labrador retriever but several tourists have appeared at the garden gate. Lucy tells them to come in and walk around, but that she's busy talking. Then she sits me down in a rump-sprung loveseat behind a cherry tree and tells me more.

Fred, it turns out, is a manager at a Fred Meyer's, a Northwest chain store that sells everything from groceries to liquor to sound equipment. "He's had the job forever," Lucy says. "He kept it because when our daughter was five, she had brain cancer, and we needed the health insurance. She had a good chance of dying. Actually, her chance of living was five percent. But we were totally honest with her. She beat it, too. She's twenty-one now."

"*Totally* honest?" I ask.

"Think about this," Lucy says intently. "We don't have much but the truth."

Whether I agree with this or not, Lucy's garden is a good place to contemplate such things—even by means of long, easy silences. I find myself really looking at the flowerbed directly in front of me. Though somewhat dormant, it's still full of color—red twigs, purple seed heads, and russet leaves in the last stage of turning.

"And red penstemons," Lucy points out. "This time of year, the garden is like a certain kind of woman, voluptuous, overblown. They're very sensual, the rhythms and changes that happen around here. It's our little paradise."

"Do you leave home much?" I ask.

"No, we don't," Lucy says. "We worked so hard to make this what it is. Our extended family is here. What it is," she says, "is a big nest."

You don't just blow into town for three days and hope to capture the Portland gardener. As if there were only one type. As if they weren't, in many crucial ways, like gardeners anywhere else. They just, however, might be more so.

I know this from talking on the phone to Dulcy Mahar, who not only covers gardening for the Portland *Oregonian*, but is the founder of the esteemed Dirty Ladies garden club.

"There was a very active garden club in my neighborhood," she tells me, "but I got kicked out for missing three meetings in a row. And I thought—a friend of mine, she'd like to be in a garden club, but she works, and another friend has a baby. I bet there's a lot of people out there missing meetings. So we founded the Dirty Ladies. We meet every third Monday at seven o'clock at night. We do no charitable works and have no teas. We even have some men who are proud to be Dirty Ladies."

There are currently thirty-five active Dirty Ladies—as opposed to the

Hardy Plant Society, which numbers nearly 1,900, Dulcy Mahar among them. "In England, hardy plants are what we call perennials," Dulcy explains. "Our climate is similar to England. Members can open their gardens to each other, and they do, and we all know each other. It's a big group, very incestuous. There's a fervor."

☙ ❈ ❧

It's immediately clear that Bruce Wakefield and Jerry Grossnickle are the most respectable people I will meet in Portland. Bruce is a corporate accountant. Jerry is chief financial officer for a tug and barge company. Both in their early forties, both wearing casual weekend clothes—unstained, somehow, by garden work—they live twelve miles northwest of Portland on a wooded road that winds along the edge of a canyon. On their five acres, they've built their dream house and garden, two acres of which is deeply wooded, and the rest of which is an unusual, emerald-lawned combination of a golf course and the Taj Mahal.

Not a speck of grime can be seen inside the house—not even inside the balsa wood *model* of the house that sits on a shelf. In the spotless kitchen, with decks and picture windows on three sides, there is nothing on the loose but the smell of pie. Center stage, on the brand new counters, is a classic *Better Homes and Gardens* home-baked pie.

Lucy knows Bruce and Jerry—they're Hardy Plant people, too—and I remember what she said about them: "Our world is inculcated by maleness. That's why I think so many great gardeners are gay men. There's an androgyny you have to feel comfortable with in order to really garden."

I don't have a chance to run this by Bruce and Jerry—and in a few minutes, androgyny is a moot point anyway. The guiding principle in this garden turns out to be harder work than I'd ever do, even if I were thrown into a prison camp to break rocks. To summarize: When Bruce and Jerry bought this five acres, all the fir trees had been logged off, but all the other trees, says Jerry, "were in here so tight you couldn't see anything. The old logging road had become a stream, and the whole plot looked like a swamp." They spent the next two years cutting out trees with a chainsaw, laying hundreds of feet of four-inch drainpipe, hauling in ton-loads of leaves, bark mulch, and granite slabs, and watching the great blue herons eat the fish they stocked in a huge pond dug by hand with small shovels.

All this was before planting began. "But I was already buying plants," says Bruce. "I was burying their pots in the ground, hauling water from downtown Portland in garbage cans."

"He's the plant one," Jerry says. "He reads himself to sleep with catalogs and plant books."

We go out onto one of the house's four decks—all of which seem to hang in the air—to look at what they finally did plant. Islands of ornamental grasses and flowers stretch out before us in a gentle slope down to the woods.

"We did what the books say," Jerry recalls. "We got out a hose, made the beds with curving edges. But from up here you can see the bigger shapes—the way the lower lawn mirrors the shape of the upper lawn—"

"Like the curve of a paisley," Bruce suggests.

"But when you really look at it, you see all of North and South America."

We start our tour in the part of the garden shaped like Texas. Seen from the ground, the variety of plants is staggering, "about a thousand different ones, I think," Bruce says, "but only eight hundred are labeled." Mountains of grass and pineapple sage, arches covered with roses, banks of nicotiana, sage, and rudbeckia—and through it all, extreme tidiness and the ribbon of lawn.

"This is our bog garden. It's Himalayan primroses and primulas. We've heard," Bruce says, trying not to sound proud, "that it's one of the best in the country."

A large pond at the bottom of the hill contains pale pink and gold fish that swim toward Bruce and Jerry when they hear their voices. "I've always threatened to bring a book down here to read and relax," Bruce says, "but I can't make it from the house to here without finding work to do."

This I can believe, especially after we enter the wooded part of the garden, with three cats gamboling behind us. Hundreds of yards are marked by a thick bark trail—laid out by Jerry one painstaking wheelbarrow load at a time.

"But it was fun," he assures me.

"Choosing which way you want the path to go," Bruce explains. "You feel like a kid playing in the woods."

"Kid stuff," Jerry agrees.

"How long did it take?" I ask.

They look at each other. "Months," Jerry says, "and I'm not really done yet, either, and then of course they'll have to be redone when the weeds come up."

This from two men whose idea of relaxation is hosting four hundred members of the Hardy Plant Society, not just for a garden tour but for refreshments, and not just once but twice a year.

"We're hardly martyrs, though," Bruce assures me.

"We're not?" Jerry counters.

"I do have a BB gun to play with," Bruce reminds him. "And we skated around on the pond last winter. We have Easter egg hunts and treasure hunts for the family." I'm relieved. Bruce and Jerry's place is an intimidatingly meticulous garden. But it is also, I realize, a yard.

❧ ☀ ☙

Margaret Willoughby's garden jumps out into the path and hits you in the face, "which is how I like it," she says. "All blowzy." Conversationally, the same thing happens with this small, round, passionately interested, elderly Australian woman. One minute after we've met, she's revealing this about prize Tasmanian hydrangeas: "My gramma used to have us all urinate in chamber pots and we'd save it up for the hydrangeas. We were sworn to secrecy."

Ensconced in a kitchen packed tight with blue-and-white china, in a neat, middle-class neighborhood, Margaret is intensely fulfilled as a gardener, except in winter, when she is fulfilled by not gardening at all. ("I light a great big fire and read a great big mystery," she says.) It's hard to find a Portland gardener who hasn't met her—she's both a Dirty Lady and a Hardy Plant Society member—and a whole legion of her neighbors has caught the habit from her.

"People come to see her garden and end up with tea, potted plants, and cuttings," says Dulcy Mahar. Margaret is a notorious over-the-fence chatter, who, even when she goes out for a walk, usually ends up meeting people and their gardens instead. She has more friends than anyone can count. (Her husband, a retired engineer eleven years her senior, has given up trying.) Margaret is sixty-six, but lately a large portion of her gardening cohorts are Generation X types, with long hair, goatees, and baggy clothes. It is not unusual, acquaintances say, to see Margaret—a neat package in clothes and neatly styled white hair—zooming around town in some kid's beat-up truck, hot on the trail of a new source of manure.

"My children say, 'Oh, Mother,'" Margaret relates, "but I'm not judg-mental. Probably because my father was extremely eccentric. He came from a very wealthy Australian family and ran away with the maid, who was my mother. When I was nine, my mother went away and never came back."

This left Margaret and two sisters to be raised in a remote Tasma-nian sheep station by their father, their grandmother, and a series of maiden aunts. "We had nine thousand acres in sheep," she recalls. "I find I can really relate to *The Thorn Birds*. We lived about ten miles from the nearest neighbor, but there were marvelous dances held in the barn, there were tennis and cricket, and we always dressed for dinner, sixteen of us at table."

As a child, Margaret was given the choice of helping either inside or outside the house—a vast 1825 convict-built mansion that had to be endlessly dusted with a dried goose wing. "I wanted to do just about anything else," Margaret remembers. She ended up working in fields of roses and tropical plants, outdoors whenever she could be, or going down to the shore to meet her father's fishing fleet. "Dad was one of the first Australians to export crayfish tails," she explains. "He had seven broth-ers, and there wasn't enough wealth to go around. He did well, but he *was* eccentric. I remember a buyer from the U.S. came and he had to take her to dinner at his club. He couldn't find his socks so he painted his ankles with black shoe polish."

Margaret formed an understandable attachment to her father and sisters, which was thrown into sharp relief when she moved to England with her first husband. "How I missed them," she recalls, "and England was so cold and dreary. Summer never seemed to come. Finally, I just came home and went to work at a cabinet and joinery store."

She had three children, a job, and garden—all of which she found reasonably satisfying until she became pen pals with Lynn Willoughby of Portland, Oregon. When the two finally met after five years of corre-spondence, it took them only six more weeks to wed. Between them, they had seven children, and they promptly produced an eighth. (The eight now range in age from twenty-five to fifty.)

Margaret took to Portland instantly, despite her confusion over the change in hemispheres and season. "I'd always had a garden, so I just thought I'd take a class," she recalls. "The first was on roses. They said you had to start with good soil and a three-foot by three-foot hole. Well, I came home and told Lynn, we have to dig big holes, dear. Well, we didn't, needless to say. My theory is, if you put some fertilizer in the bottom of the hole it will all be okay, even if it's just a small hole. Besides, it's all experimentation, anyway. You can all live in the same town and buy the same plant and it lives for some and dies for others."

In any case, Margaret refuses to be dependent, even on her husband. She'd rather have all the space (a double city lot, crammed full) to herself. "Lynn does the chipping and shredding, but I find you fight over the land. Now, Dulcy's husband, Ted—he doesn't know a sunflower from a pansy. It's better that way."

Nevertheless, Lynn has indulged Margaret's weakness for unusual birdhouses and garden sculpture. Two years ago, in Vancouver, he bought her a carved wooden figurehead, which she promptly nailed to a tree. When he retired, he bought her a hothouse. We go out to see it, past a gigantic weathered brass bell that hangs from the eaves of the patio.

"This is just like the bell my gramma used to call us in from playing," she says, "so when I saw it, I had to have it. It's a bit of Australiana." So is the garden itself, she says, with its twining trumpet vines, wisteria, and climbing roses, and tomatoes growing among the flowers. There is a semiformal herb garden with thick lavender hedges, and a bird bath hidden in every shrub. At the back of the lot, near Lynn's compost and shredding area, is an old wood stove—"not for decoration," Margaret says, "but so I can make myself a cup of tea. Why should I have to go indoors? I find it so funny when people look at this garden and say, 'Oh, it must be hard work.' Oh, no, I reply, I've worked inside—that's *work*."

In fact, in November and December, Margaret runs an indoor business. With a friend, she produces dried flower and evergreen wreaths which are sold in a big barn ten miles east of Portland. "I like American Christmas," Margaret says. "A lovely great dinner and a huge fire. I never did understand going to the beach on December twenty-fifth." More important, the dried flower business supports her gardening habit, and that, she says, she could not live without.

"It relaxes me," she says. "You can get out there and dig away and forget all your troubles. I remember visiting a mental hospital where they were giving shock treatments, and I suggested to the doctor that perhaps all these disturbed people could just garden. The doctor told me some people can't stand dirt under their fingernails. I suppose," she says, trying to be open-minded, "that could be true."

Margaret's current best friends, a male couple in their thirties who live twenty blocks away, don't understand the dirty fingernail thing either. "Danny and Wayne are a bit reclusive," Margaret says. "They don't like odd people dropping by." She looks at me for a moment. "I suppose I mean *the odd person* dropping by. You're odd enough, but they won't care."

❧ ☀ ☙

Any real estate agent would tell you that most people are looking for the house they spent the best part of their childhood in—which accounts for some people's passionate attachment to rock solid 1940s' ranch houses, while others feel more secure in Victorian warrens of tiny rooms and gingerbread. When I see Wayne and Danny's house, which sits on an unkempt acre of garden and weeds, a sense of homecoming washes over me.

It is large and wooden, with two stories, simple turn-of-the-century lines, porches, big, uncomplicated windows—and every painted surface is either white or the gray-blue of shadows. It feels unfinished—on its way up or down from wreckage. Two big, paint-peeling barns sit behind it. The doors of one are open, with yellow light and bombastic operetta music streaming out. Above the lintel is a big sign that reads: Lonesomeville.

I get out of the car into a cloud of damp, maritime air. Wayne Hills and Danny Hughes' house, I decide, is the West Coast twin of my mother's house in Hampton Bays, Long Island. A light goes on in the living room. I see a white wall with a large sculpted swordfish hanging on it. It looks very much like the three-inch tattoo on my back.

Meanwhile Margaret has walked under a leaning trellis into the yard, and Wayne, a thin man in paint-spattered clothes and hair that looks like someone has attacked it with hedge clippers, is flinging himself into her arms.

"How *did* you get this unusual salmon color into these roses?" Margaret asks him.

"Poop," he answers. "Human Portland poop at five bucks a truckload. It works wonderful. How do you like my new, professional haircut?"

"It looks like you just got out of prison."

"You don't think it looks manly—in a boyish way?"

"No. Now let me explain to you about Robin."

Wayne was not expecting *the odd person*. He gives me a guarded look. In lieu of saying something, I show him my tattoo.

"Hey!" he says, "that's just like Danny's—"

"I know," I say. "I couldn't believe it."

He takes me into Lonesomeville, where his partner, Danny, also paint-stained, but with long, curly black hair, is making furniture, sculpture, masks, and birdhouses. He and Margaret are delighted to see each other, and he spends the next half hour with her in the garden, discussing plants and flowers I can barely see in the failing light. I get the impression, though, that the flower beds have been dug deeply, but never smoothed into a mound. Instead, wildly healthy roses, daisies, lythrum, and delphiniums tangle from big clods of earth.

"Why Lonesomeville?" I ask Wayne.

"Oh, that's our little joke on the world," he says. "We're anything but lonesome around here. Come and see the house."

He shows me into the kitchen of my dreams—an enormous room with black-and-white linoleum and lobsters stencilled everywhere, 1930s' china in the cupboards, ancient appliances whirring comfortingly. A large, ratty armchair sits in a corner below two wide-open windows, through which the wonderful damp air blows.

"That's where you curl up and have coffee tomorrow morning," Wayne tells me.

"Nine?" I say.

"Oh, ten," he replies.

Seated in the ratty armchair the next morning, I sink directly into the scene—as if Wayne and Danny and I are, on some level, related. At the same time, I know I will leave here exhausted from it all. There is no privacy. We are going to discuss everything—which, says Wayne, I should view as a compliment. "I would rather dig a hole and fill it with manure than talk to most people," he says.

"People don't bother me," I say. "I like them."

"But *why*?" Wayne says.

"Why gardening?" I counter.

"Oh, we love gardening," Danny says. "Despite the Hardy Plant Society."

"What's wrong with the Hardy Plant Society?"

"Nothing. It's just everyone doing everything in groups," Wayne says. "We don't mix with them at all. Ever. When I met Danny, it changed my life. I realized: you don't *have* to live in a group, you don't *have* to be a consumer. You don't have to obey the rules—some rules are ridiculous. I mean, in Portland it's illegal to have a chicken, but not a pit bull. What made *that* happen? The great chicken rampage of ought-six?"

Out in the garden, the opinions continue to fly. Danny lays out his basic principles:

"We're not interested in fussy. You divide the ones that do well and forget the pissy ones that die. We don't go crazy with water, either—that's why Rome fell. Also, we don't deadhead. A garden shouldn't look like spring when it's not."

Wayne and Danny's front yard is alive with flowers, all of them ranging about the yard in their low-water way. On the side of the house, in the middle of a wet, green rock garden, a subtle waterfall pours four inches from one hollowed-out log onto another. I begin to notice unusually simple, rustic trellises, a lot of them made from twigs, most of them asymmetrical. And then there are waist-high fences, twiggy and skeletal, for holding roses in, or floppy perennials up.

"I call them girdles," Danny says. "There isn't a piece of garden furniture I haven't reinvented."

This turns out to be true. Chairs, benches, birdhouses, fences, and trellises are scattered all over the yard, even in the quarter acre devoted to canaries and "whatever the hell wants to grow there."

"I was a legal assistant downtown," Wayne recalls. "At the end of my days there, I smelled like a lawyer. Danny scooped cookie dough at Mrs. Field's."

"I'd been to art school, but that was a joke," Danny says.

"Fine art," Wayne says, "is the emperor's new clothes."

"It's crap."

"It's white wine and Brie cheese."

"It sucks," Danny concludes. "Anyway, we met at the gym. It was pure lust."

"Then we went to dinner and talked and talked, and then it was love."

They moved into the Lonesomeville house, which Wayne had bought cheaply, in a "trashed" state. Danny thought it was beautiful. Knowing nothing about gardening at all, he planted a few daylilies. "Then I peeled back the weeds to see what was underneath and I got hooked," he recalls. Shortly after that came Margaret Willoughby's first serendipitous visit. Soon, she was bringing them seeds, cuttings, plants. The garden grew exponentially.

Oddly, so did both Wayne and Danny's careers. Together, they began building folk art birdhouses and garden trellises, and despite their distaste for the art world, their wares have sold amazingly well. Danny's tropical-theme furniture, sculptures, and masks have become popular, not just on the West Coast, but in resort areas from Aspen to Jamaica. First Danny quit his job, then Wayne. Lonesomeville products are now sold at 150 retail outlets, as well as to private homes and galleries.

"But how?" I ask. "You guys can be so snotty."

"Oh, I'm a lot nicer than Wayne," Danny says. "I have manners. That actually helps. I just sold four masks at a thousand dollars each."

"We are *building this life*," Wayne says. "With two hands. That's all that matters, do you see that? Find the person you love, drink lots of water, have lots of sex, grow lots of flowers, do you see that?"

❧ ✺ ☙

At Millie's place, I search in vain for the substandard goldfish pond that gave Penny Vogel her start.

"I had two grandsons, ages two and three," she tells me, "and they loved to play in that muddy, dirty water, but it wasn't safe." She asked her landlord if she could fill it in—perhaps plant a few pansies in the fill-dirt.

Her landlord was Millie Kiggins, now seventy-six—a lifelong farmer Dulcy Mahar refers to as "the original Tugboat Annie." Her forty acres near Estacada—a logging and farming town thirty miles southeast of Portland—have been in her family since 1913. Her great delight in this ancestral land is obvious—she still likes to spend her time driving around it on a tractor, followed by dogs, dressed comfortably in overalls, thermal underwear, and workboots. A few pansies, she thought—why not?

But something came over Penny when she planted those pansies. They looked pleasing next to the old red climbing rose that was already there. "I've always gardened, to a degree," she says, "but more for vegetables and canning." For some reason, at the age of forty-eight, in a rented house with a rented yard, she suddenly began tearing up the soil in pursuit of the ultimate English cottage garden. She and her husband had planned to move to Estacada just temporarily. He would take a brief job in the logging industry, they'd save their money, and then go back to their home in Washington State. But that did not stop Penny from planting a full acre in perennial flowers, roses, shrubs, and vines.

"Millie thought I was a little crazy," she recalls. It didn't keep her from helping Penny—there were lots of rocks to haul, lots of mulch to return to the soil. "We're both, as it turns out, very strong," Penny says. "Millie's not into the planting or planning, and if she's supposed to stand on a rock, she'll stand on a plant and squash it, but she liked to see it all take shape, and soon we were working together most of the day."

Gardening isn't all the two women have in common. There is also a love of books and an unfulfilled urge to travel. They believe dogs belong in a garden. They believe the older you get, the more you should do, look, and say exactly what you want. It was an auspicious pairing. That first year, Penny's husband suffered a stroke and became an invalid, their plans to return to Washington were scrapped, and Penny stayed on at Millie's invitation.

That was six years ago. The garden, now five acres in size and known to Hardy Plant people all over Oregon as Kinzy Faire—or simply Millie's place—is now almost an attraction. It has its own informal gift shop, where Millie's primitive—and sometimes humorous—birdhouses are sold. In the summer, you can often find Lucy and Fred Hardiman, or Margaret and Lynn Willoughby, or all four, sitting under the pine trees among the ferns, trading stories with Millie, while Penny listens contentedly.

What they discuss is hardly limited to gardening, but there have been in-depth talks about exactly what constitutes an English cottage garden. Penny thinks it means "vines, shrubs, perennials, fruit trees, all closely mixed. The style came from common people," she says, "and if they had it, they grew it. I like to play with color, for instance, but if a plant volunteers, I just can't pull it out. If it's there, it's there. I'm a pretty casual gardener."

In old Keds, jeans, and a sweatshirt, she looks the part. "How many hours do you spend out here?" I ask.

"Oh, all day," she says easily. "I try to get my housework done before the sun comes up, and I won't go out to work in the rain. If it starts raining while I'm out there, though, I'll stay. I don't try to change the soil to neutral, or anything like that. I don't have time to coddle. I grow what grows. I used to quilt. I think of this as a kind of quilt."

Colors here do seem to fall into related clumps—blue balloon flower, thistle, and delphinium; coreopsis, daisies, and marigolds; a spread of yellow-orange ground cover beneath the Joseph's Coat rose, with all its fiery variations. Penny is the only gardener who's ever given me a good answer to the stupid question *Do you have a favorite color?*

"If I had to limit it," she says, "I'd go with yellow and white year-round, early spring to late fall. Let's see . . . snowdrops, feverfew, tulips, crocus, pansies, and you could have daffodils, of course. Maybe then white grape hyacinth, Stella d'Oro lilies, euphorbia, coreopsis, marigolds, daisies—and then, oh, how about salvia and aster for just a little blue? Oh, and a Gertrude Jekyll rose, which is worth it just for the smell."

We walk the curved bark paths of the garden, many of which are dotted with volunteer seedlings Penny refuses to uproot. "They're babies," she says. "You have to grow them at least until you recognize what they are. You don't get babies at all if you're too neat, you know, and you can't duplicate how nature spreads them in the garden. Oh," she says happily, "there's nothing I love like a self-seeder."

As we walk through the flower beds, we climb a gradual hill. At the top is a tiny chapel Millie built three years ago, in honor of the grandparents who first homesteaded this land. Occasional weddings and sunrise services are held here, but mostly, Penny says, it's for "sitting quietly and feeling good."

"And Millie thought that was a good enough idea that she just built the place?"

"Yes, that's how she is," Penny says. "Last fall, she decided to go away and drive around the country, and I thought that was a wonderful idea. We just went! When I told my husband, he was a bit shocked. We were gone for two and a half months. We went through Montana, Colorado, Arizona, we were in Washington, D.C., and Tennessee and New Mexico and Georgia. We just went. We both like history and we don't like touristy. We got along perfectly."

So well that at the end of the trip, Millie, who'd been married briefly in the forties but never had a child, asked Penny to become her legally adopted daughter. "I loved the idea," she recalls. "I asked my real mother, of course, but we all eventually decided that you can't have too many mothers. These have become the best days of my life. Not only do I have the family I always had—I'm getting acquainted with a family I just acquired."

"Where is Millie, anyway?" I ask. At intervals, I've seen her at the top of a rise, in her tractor—but she's seemed too busy, or too shy, to talk much.

"Actually, she hurt her leg in a rototiller accident," Penny tells me. "It was pretty bad. I hope she's in her house with her feet up, reading. She needs to take it easy."

"What about you?" I ask. "What do you need?"

"Just to hang out," Penny answers. "Discipline I'm not good at. I love it the way it is right now in the garden, knowing that Millie's happy, and hearing the sounds of nature, hundreds of birds, dogs running around—minus the airplane, maybe. And me working in the garden."

"What do you think about?"

"Nothing at all. Which gives me incredible peace. I don't arrange," she says happily. "I just grow."

11 What People Keep

Some flourish
for us, some hide their weed
identity till networked
into place. By then
no spade uproots them. By then
they have entered the language.

LOIS BEEBE HAYNA, "SEEDS AS THEY FALL"

Just after the Fourth of July, I get a call from Will

Eddings's neighbor Jerri Brackett. A naturally nosy woman, she has been spying on his yard. She wants me to know what's going on there.

"That yard he works in, it used to be nothing but bare dirt," Jerri says. "There wasn't even a blade of grass. And every morning, he's out planting those morning glories. When they bloom, his place will be to die for." There is a bare silence. "That was stupid," she says, laughing nervously. "I mean, he has AIDS. He *is* dying."

I find the garden without much trouble. In it, Will Eddings, a gaunt, thirty-nine-year-old man with ropy muscles and a buzz-cut, is transplanting coleus. "I thought I was going to be one of those miracle people," he says. "I thought the chemo wouldn't make me sick. But then I got nauseous and my muscles started contracting, and I thought the hell with it. My doctor told me to go home and play in my garden."

That was on March 10—two months before Denver's last frost date. Will went into his yard and began planting anyway, even though it was too soon.

"I did not care," Will recalls. "I knew the soil was ready. I could see it waiting. I knew within a month we would be eating salads."

He was right to persevere—the lettuce came up before anyone else's was sown. Since then, Will hasn't eaten much else. Thirty pounds underweight and plagued by stomach trouble, he won't be able to eat tomatoes this August, but he grows them for his companion, Keith Vogt, who's HIV-positive but healthy. In return, Keith cares for Will, which sometimes means attending to his most basic bodily needs, but most of the time entails hauling around sacks of topsoil and chunks of salvaged flagstone.

"I like him to help me," Will says, "but not too much. This is my garden."

It is a front-yard garden, the kind you see while walking by on the sidewalk. Other houses on this street—what remains of a once-fancy

Victorian neighborhood near downtown—have threadbare grass or worn-out junipers. Will's garden is crammed with corn, broccoli, okra, lettuce, seven kinds of tomatoes, and the year's fifth sowing of spinach. In the middle of it all sits a garden bench, salvaged in an alley and covered with a wire trellis, up which red morning glories are beginning to twine. "I have no big plan for this garden," Will says. "I'm just going to keep on planting."

Not a big plan, his doctor tells me, until you consider that gardening is what keeps Will alive. He is still being treated medically, but it's come down to a question of what to live for, and even that won't work forever.

"I'm starting to meet with a psychologist so we can talk about dying," Will tells me, from the garden bench where he has collapsed. "I'm starting to know it's going to happen, whether I walk out in the street and get hit by a bus or this gets me. I'm trying to prepare for death, but I still think, what the hell, I'm just supposed to let it go?"

We watch a line of afternoon rain move across the street toward us. Will rouses himself and begins to talk about his past. Keith comes to the window, motions him in out of the rain. Will waves him away. He will stay outside while he can.

Growing up in the Sacramento Valley, and later, as a society hairdresser in San Francisco and Dallas, Will lived luxuriously until 1986, when the HIV virus he'd contracted years ago mutated into AIDS and forced him to give up working. It was only then, living with Keith in a rented house with a hard-packed dirt yard, that he considered gardening for the first time. "I had been on disability for so long, and in the summer I just laid out in the sun and read books," he recalls. "But I had never been content that way, and I started with tomatoes, chives, spinach, and a little radicchio. Oh and I *worked* it," he recalls fondly. "What is a garden without weeds?"

He kept on going until early winter that year, and the next year he quadrupled the garden. Each year after that, he worked the land from frost to frost, always cleaning up meticulously in the fall. "It's windy here," he explains. "Things just blow in and grow all over if you don't keep them tidy. I mean, look at this," he says, showing me seedlings in the seams between two flagstones. "Portulaca has blown in from somewhere. And these white pansies, they just showed up, too."

This is what Will has been meaning to tell me, even though he's covered with cold sweat, and *must*, Keith insists, come in for a rest.

"The winds," Will insists. "In winter, the winds come through here so hard, and seeds from my garden will fly all over this neighborhood, further than we can see. They'll blow, and I'll still be here."

In the spring, they'll sprout, and who will tend them? *Will you be alive next summer?* is a difficult question to ask.

I don't have to. "Keith will take care of this garden," Will says. "He knows I will come back from the grave and slap him if he doesn't."

November

I went by Will's garden just before the first blizzard of the year came down from the west. Seeds were blowing everywhere, just as he had hoped. Keith had to move away a few weeks after Will died—living on one disability check instead of two made it impossible for him to afford the rent. I could not tell if the new tenants intended to maintain the garden. If Will was looking down at that moment—"looking down" was an image he seemed to appreciate—he was appalled at the trash on the sidewalk he always kept swept, mortified at the ragged state of his planting beds, but exhilarated at the terrible cold wind. A sunflower seed rattled as it flew past.

My sphere is narrow these days, and as the days get shorter it gets smaller. I have been invited on an outing to cut down a Christmas tree, but I don't go. I can see December 21, the shortest day of the year, homing in. I dread the lensing down of light.

This year, for the first time, I took some care about putting the garden to bed. I covered my lily beds with leaves and burlap sacking, bricks at each edge to keep them from blowing away. I tied up the rose bush canes to keep the snow from snapping them. I clipped the hedges and buried wood ash by the lilacs. There are still leaves to collect and dig into the soil.

I didn't preserve a single cell from my summer garden. No cans of salsa, no roasted chile, no jam, no pickles, no dried flower wreath, no basil in the freezer. It wasn't because I had decided to scale back. Instead, I just forgot, and that bothers me.

As a woman, comma. As a woman, comma, I hate that phrase. But right now I am drawn to the specific company of women, the older the better.

The first older woman I talk to is a witch. A good witch—the first thing Margaret Johnson does is offer me chocolate. "Leftover from the chocolate frenzy," she explains. "I started it five years ago. It's a third-degree pagan initiation, and we were just at a pagan festival, so . . ."

"Can I ask what else goes on at the chocolate frenzy?"

"No," she says pleasantly.

Margaret Johnson has long, curly red-blonde hair, big glasses that make her green eyes even bigger, and a teenage body in a big sweater and jeans. She sits cross-legged on a kitchen chair. She is fifty. We are talking, for the second time, in her standard, middle-class kitchen, in her standard middle-class neighborhood. On the plastic tablecloth there is a philodendron planted in a plastic pot. Family pictures are crammed in everywhere. There is even a needlepoint sampler that reads *Home Is Where the Heart Is.* If it weren't for the baskets overflowing with drying herbs, this could be the home of a Mary Kay saleswoman. It is not like any coven I ever read about.

"Well," Margaret laughs, "people misunderstand The Craft. I am a witch and I practice Witch Craft, but one thing I *don't* do is worship the Devil or harm little animals. We are not satanists. The satanists, in fact, think we're wimps and pansies."

The first time I came here it was summer, and I left loaded down with garden loot: lettuce, tomatoes, cilantro, peppers, round lemon cucumbers, and eggplants. Margaret also gave me Indian sweetgrass for braiding, basil for cooking, patchouli to bring me prosperity, and oregano to hang upside down in my kitchen so that the oils would flow towards its head as it dried. She gave me hyssop, mint, and lavender for a bath.

I was happy and overwhelmed. "I'll make a love potion," I joked.

"Don't do that," she said, quite seriously. "If you do that, you're taking someone else's love, and you shouldn't do that. If you want to make a potion"—and the look she gave me clearly indicated that I might want to know what I was doing before I tried—"make one that says *I can do this love thing, but I don't need to control.*"

I went home and made spaghetti sauce instead. And since then, whenever I think of Margaret Johnson, I get an image of the summer sun burning onto her small, intensively cultivated garden, where the herbs flourish and the only prevailing moral code is *Think for yourself*. I wonder how Margaret will appear in winter, when nothing blooms. What she does is burn sage from her garden. "You strip off the flowers and the leaves," she says, doing so. "Then you make them into a kind of ball." She drops the ball into an abalone shell, lights it, and waves the sweet smoke into the air with a fan made of raptor feathers. "Now, stand up," she orders. "Shut your eyes, breathe, and take your baseball hat off. Breathe in that smoke, and the spirits will take all that anxiety and sleeplessness away. Here," she concludes, stuffing dried sage into a plastic Safeway bag. "Take all this home and use it a lot. You need cleansing. Now, what did you want to ask me?"

I add the Safeway bag to the herb book and the custom-made herbal bath mixture she's already given me. "I want to know how you feel in winter," I say.

"I feel good," she says. "I always bring a little of the earth inside. Like this patchouli plant—it's inside, or it would die. And all the herbs I dry. It's good to have them with me in winter. There's a plant for every problem there is, you know."

Margaret has been sifting through plants and problems almost all her life. She grew up in the most urban part of Denver, "a lot of asphalt," she remembers, but her grandparents were North Carolina transplants, and her grandmother treated all her colds with herbal teas and poultices. Married at nineteen, she followed her husband to Beaufort, South Carolina, where he was trained for Vietnam and subsequently shipped over. For the next three years, she worked in a small hospital, "washing dead bodies, delivering babies, everything" and learned gardening at the feet of her landlord, a seventy-year-old woman who chopped wood and dug sassafras roots for tea.

"It was very rural," she recalls. "The trees all had long thorns, alligators came into the garden. I had swarming termites, spiders bigger than my hand. I screamed a lot. Snakes fell on my head. Nature is one thing—snakes are another. But tomatoes grew wild, and I had gooseberries, onions, bell peppers, cucumbers, and eggplant and I liked watching it grow."

In the late sixties she came back to Denver, got a job as a switchboard operator, separated from her husband, and grew disenchanted with the Mormon faith she'd adopted at sixteen.

"A woman I was working with was taking pagan classes," she recalls. "It threatened me terribly, but I was intrigued. My religion always made it very clear what was bad, but I felt there must be more than knowing what bad was. I was well programmed into thinking I was going to hell, but I was never sure if that made sense."

In pagan classes, Margaret came to believe that bad merely meant un-Christian and that the Devil was "a purely Christian deity," as opposed to the "ancient god of the woods, or Pan, who had great stag horns and brought fertility and magical sex between the God and the Goddess." Pagan, she discovered, merely means "person of the land."

And that is what she has been for the past twenty years. For the last five, she's had her own coven—a sort of witch study group—and she and her husband spend most of the summer at pagan festivals or in the garden. In this religion you can't not garden.

"Dirt is not just a dead thing," she tells me. "Touching the ground is a sacred thing. Feel this."

A light piece of flannel stuffed with lavender descends onto my eyes, with its wonderful smell. "Allow the herbs to calm you," Margaret orders. "From time immemorial," she continues, while I lie with my head back on the sofa, "people have used herbs in winter to make sleeping sachets, little bags that you stuff with herbs and put under your pillow to dream of your future husband. Or wife, but it's mostly women who care about these things."

I hear her walking into the next room. "Personally, I make sachets for people to carry around with them," she yells. "I just made one for a friend who is deathly afraid of airplanes. I put in calming herbs and special stones." She comes back into the room and opens the front door. A blast of cold wind blows through the kitchen, and I sit up straighter. "Whether or not an herb or a stone can keep a plane from falling out of the sky," she says, whipping off the lavender so she can look me in the eye, "my friend trusted that I made it with love. And it worked."

ᘒ ☼ ᘓ

A few days later, I take my daughter, Coco, to western Nebraska, in search of farm wives who still put up their crops in mason jars. I am not at all sure I will find them. Most of my Nebraska contacts live in Denver now, and consider it a step up. Even their Nebraska relatives seem happy to have given up the more labor-intensive kinds of farm and ranch work for whatever fun happens to come through town. Oshkosh, Nebraska, the town I'm headed for, has a wilder reputation than most prairie towns of less than a thousand people. No less than six bridge clubs are in full swing—and full rivalry—and few of the women in town have forgotten the brief season when someone's relative came to town, opened an actual French cafe, and imported male strippers once a week.

"Oh, it was exciting," says Marcia Bunger, who was trying to escape from an abusive husband at the time. "It was sexual discrimination in reverse, and I know I shouldn't have enjoyed it, but oh, I did."

Marcia lives in Denver now, but her affection for Oshkosh has not diminished. Finally, after several hours of phoning, she finds me the last of the old school canners—Donna Zoucha, a sixty-nine-year-old farm wife who has lived in Garden County all her life and learned gardening and canning from her mother. "I have such warm memories of Donna," Marcia tells me. "She could handle just about anything—children, chickens, anything. And what a card shark she is."

We pull up to Donna's place on a November afternoon with ice in the air. Donna and her husband, George, have moved into town from the family ranch they still call the Home Place. It is a modest white frame house with a sixty-by-sixty-foot garden, perfectly plowed under into straight rows.

"I put a marigold or a seed dahlia at the head of each row so that's what you see from the street," Donna says. "People here have a lot of pride—at least when it comes to outdoors. In summer, my house gets neglected drastically. One gal in my bridge club, she says, 'Why don't you budget your time?' But I say to her, 'Everyone drives by and sees my lawn and garden, they don't see inside my house.' So that's what I keep spiffied.'"

We walk around Donna's scrupulous lawn, entirely free of dandelions at no small cost to her, inspect her raspberry canes, and wonder if the elephant garlic is sprouting. Her tightly curled gray hair whips in the wind. She is dressed for labor, in polyester pants, matching shirt, and sensible shoes. She is not one for aimless strolling.

"Everything in this garden is eaten or canned," she tells me. "I still don't buy much at the store but flour, sugar, cinnamon, coffee, and salt. George brings in beef from the ranch, and I still keep chickens. With the children gone, we can't eat as much as we used to, but I still can excessively, you could say."

That's what comes of growing up on the Home Place. "There was eleven of us kids," she recalls. "We had to have a vegetable garden. My father would turn over five acres and plant it in sweet corn, green beans,

195

melons, and squash. We hoed, pulled weeds, and picked. We did our watering with a bucket."

Donna's mother canned hundreds of quarts of vegetables, pickles, and jam and the children were expected to help. Donna never saw it as drudgery. "Most of all, I remember drying the sweet corn," Donna says. "We'd blanch it on the cob, cool it, and cut it, cover the dining room table with an old sheet, and lay the corn out on it for several days. Then Mother would sew it into cloth bags and hang it on the clothesline, and when you walked past, you were supposed to hit the sacks with a stick. We made creamed corn from that all winter."

As a child, Donna ran constantly, up and down from the attic for cans of dried corn and flour, down to the cellar for canned vegetables for dinner—or to escape a tornado. "Two of my sisters were killed that way," she recalls. "I was three at the time and they were eight and nine. You never saw it coming, it was just a wall of dirt, and the school where they were at was a mile northeast. Boards were flying, I guess, and that's what killed them."

We go inside, so that Donna can show me her winter stores. Her husband watches TV in the living room, kept company by a parrot who does an uncanny imitation of a military bugle. Donna's kitchen is piled with supplies—jars of honey stacked up, dried anasazi beans from her own garden and her neighbor's, boxes of spices for pickle making. The only clue that she ever rests is a dog-eared copy of a romance novel called *Dueling Hearts*.

"But this is nothing compared to what I did when my five kids were home," she protests. "Just as soon as the green beans started coming, in mid-July, I started in canning *something* every day, even if it were only four quarts of dill pickles or six quarts or so of beets. I used to figure I needed a hundred quarts each of beans and tomatoes to last a winter, a hundred more of fruit. Carrots I'd put in a glass jar and fill it with sand. Pickles, oh gosh, thirty to fifty quarts, and at least a hundred pints of jam."

Her three daughters, she is proud to say, still take on some of this themselves—using water bath canners, sieves, and jars handed down by their grandmothers on both sides. "And I still have my gramma's recipe box," she says, handing me a small wooden box with dovetail joints crammed full of newspaper clippings, scribbled recipes, and ancient correspondence.

I pull out a recipe at random—creamed corn for a crowd, it seems.

"Take one gallon dried corn," it begins. The next twenty or so are all for basic sweets: *burnt sugar cake, white cake, plain cake, caramel filling for pie*.

Then I strike a vein of faded letters, written in a spidery hand in the thirties. "And I held up my hand to be saved," I read. "Oh it was such a fine place and such wonderful people . . ."

"I cook with these recipes all the time," Donna says. "And I do just like my grandmother did—you don't pay attention, you throw it together, it comes out perfect every time. Have you ever had whole wheat bread with sand cherry jelly? We would go into the sand hills and find the bushes with their branches kind of laying down, the berries ripening under the sand. There's a very large pit, like a chokecherry. I just strain them and wash them good. The flavor is luscious."

She sets a pint down in front of my daughter, who immediately begins trying to break the vacuum seal. The sand cherry jelly is the bright red of Kool-Aid. Next to it, Donna places a quart jar containing what looks like a human elbow.

"Hardly no one cans chicken anymore," she explains proudly. "It's just cut up, raw, a breast and a thigh or a wing or a back, and you process it and keep it on hand for luscious chicken-rice casseroles. It's the perfect thing to bring over when there's a death in the family."

Coco and I just look at each other. Without speaking, we are of one mind on this—the jelly comes with us, the chicken stays here.

"Five o'clock and dark already," Donna observes, getting up to draw the curtains.

"Why do you still do all this?" I ask Donna. "Do you really need to?"

"No," she says, "but it does taste better. I was talking to my son's wife last month and I says, what do you need out there in California that you don't have? And she says she would like one quart of my home-canned tomato juice for spaghetti sauce. *One quart!* I sent five, because there wasn't much room on the plane. But in a month's time it was gone. I suppose," she says, "it gives me a sense of security."

                     ꙮ

I am trying to tell Lois Hayna about Donna Zoucha, but I am distracted by green. Against a backdrop of abundant scented geraniums in pots, Lois Hayna is sitting backlit by sun, wearing a wonderful, flowing, dark green silk shirt with green leggings and looking at me with her attentive, interested eyes, which are also green. She listens like a bird, her head cocking to the side from time to time. She exudes the kind of absolute alertness I seldom see in anyone, much less a woman of seventy-nine.

She balks, though, at being called youthful. Her eyesight prevents her from driving at night, she points out, bending over is harder than it used to be, and she has no compunctions about death, which she alludes to now and then, casually, without a trace of fear.

"In the garden," she says at one point, "I don't waste space or energy or time. I don't *have* that much time."

Lois Hayna is a poet first, a gardener second, everything else somewhere further down the line. It took decades to get things set up the way she wants them, and she is not about to make concessions now. She does not, for instance, speak the litany I have come to expect from female gardeners everywhere: *Sorry my house is such a mess. I guess I'm more interested in working outside.*

"I've certainly heard it said before," Lois tells me. "When I was younger, if a woman gardened, or played the piano or had *any* interest other than being house-proud, women would say 'Yes, she plays beautifully, but you should see her house, it's a wreck.' It got so that when someone kept their house beautifully, I felt like saying 'Yes, but have you ever heard her play the piano?'"

In rural northern Wisconsin, in the 1920s, Lois's mother apologized for her garden instead of her house. "If one row was uneven, she felt awful," Lois recalls. "She let the house be a mess, but that garden was important. It fed us, after all."

Lois's father was a railroad man. He disappeared when Lois, the eldest of three, was ten, leaving the family dependent on whatever they could grow or can from the garden and "some kind of county welfare." These hard times may have changed Lois's mother's philosophy. "I think she had the beginnings of a feminist attitude," Lois says. "She didn't know how to make it happen, but she didn't think it was right that all a girl could do was teach, or be a secretary, and that to do anything you had to have a man supporting you."

Lois had no intention of doing any of that. Almost from the moment she learned to read, she spent hours in her room, writing down "poems and poems, terrible stuff," accused by her mother of being antisocial. The Wisconsin town she lived in was so small she had to leave home to attend high school, boarding during the week with three other girls from tiny towns. Ecstatic to have been given a scholarship, she entered the

University of Wisconsin at Madison in 1933. "Right in the middle of the Depression," she recalls, "and it wasn't all bad. Everyone was poor, everyone was desperate for a job, and that made me not quite the exception. I was publishing a few poems, too. Nobody paid me, but that's standard. They always act as if they're doing you a great favor."

The terms of her scholarship specified that Lois attend home economics classes, but she found every possible way around them and was always thrilled that no one pegged her as one of "those Home Ec types." Once in graduate school, she thought, she'd be a poet type, nothing more and nothing less.

"But instead, I got married to a man from Mississippi," she relates. "Money was tight, and I started having children. I had three in three years. I hated Mississippi. My mother-in-law insisted on showing me the place in her Bible where it said that colored people aren't even human beings, and all the women my age were these Southern belles who had got their man and now they did not know *what* to do with themselves."

Lois kept her spirits by striking up friendships with "foreigners," painting what she remembers as substandard watercolors, and dreaming of writing poetry. When all three children were in school, she thought, she'd have blocks of time to herself. "But the marriage was rocky," she recalls, "and that's when we moved to Denver. Southerners do not transplant well. Six weeks after we got here, my husband announced he was leaving us. I looked for a job. I got one in an insurance company, and I got my children off to school." A new phase began, one which included neither poetry nor a social life. "In this world you are *supposed* to be married," Lois theorizes. "Life is all about couples and children, and the hormones do get in the way. You make up your mind to do without men, but they get past you somehow and wreck all your plans."

This happened in the late forties. In the late fifties, another brief chance came and went. With her youngest child halfway through high school, Lois married again—an electrical engineer named Joe Hayna. When her youngest left for college, she decided, she'd quit her job to write full-time.

"Right about that time, my middle child married, had a baby, and came home six weeks later," Lois continues. "My daughter had to go to work and I had to watch the baby. So I was caught again, until that child went to school. And this is when I started gardening. And of course I went *much* too deeply into it."

The Haynas had bought a house on a half acre in the Denver suburb of Wheat Ridge. When Lois went out to use the land, she did so not to feed her family, but to investigate the mystery of herbs, which had always fascinated her.

"In my mother's garden, herbs were extraneous," she explains. "It was too important to grow food. I didn't know a thing about herbs, and there were so many to try. At one point I grew three-hundred-and-twenty different kinds. It was always so interesting to see what would come up out of a seed. And it was something I could do with my granddaughter, because all kids love dirt and water, especially mixed together."

Lois became what she likes to call a casual herbist. "In other words, nothing has to be perfect and it doesn't have to take all your time," she says. "I was interested in what they looked like and what you could do with them." She taught herself to cook with herbs—"That soup on the stove right now is *well* flavored with rosemary and thyme"—and combed her local library for references to herbs—medicinal, poisonous, or literary.

"A lot of these herbal remedies are amusing," she says. "When you read enough about it, you see that a certain herb can cure loose teeth, and sores, and fever. I used to wonder how one plant could do all that. Finally I realized that all those things are symptoms of scurvy. And you have to realize that whole populations would subsist on nothing but grains all winter, and the first green things that came up would be so welcome. No wonder herbs got such a reputation."

With her poetry still on hold, Lois slowly began to write a book on herbs that would take her more than thirty years to finish. And she kept on growing herbs. Finally, after twenty-seven years of gardening, Lois and Joe sold their land to move south to Colorado Springs, and it was time to decide what to keep. Their new yard would be smaller, and Lois's time would finally be devoted to writing poetry.

"I decided only to grow what I use and love," she recalls. "Savory, sage, salad burnet, wild marjoram, oregano, angelica, garlic chives, and chives. Oh, and I have to have basil. Sweet marjoram, too." All these grow in her new, smaller yard—and on the windowsill in winter. "Don't forget scented geraniums," she says, rubbing their fuzzy leaves between her fingers. "Technically, they are herbs. And rosemary, of course. Are you acquainted with rosemary?"

She breaks off a two-inch stalk and hands it to me. I crumble it to release the scent and split the crumbs between the two front pockets of my jeans. If Lois Hayna, having grown 320 different herbs, chose this one to give me, I intend to smell it the rest of this day.

Joe Hayna died seven years ago, and since then Lois has been delightedly selfish. She gives readings, visits the public schools to cast the magic of poetry over children, and pops in and out of writers' colonies. At one recent workshop, she says, a much younger female poet said: "But Lois, you write so much about wind!"

"And cold, and North, and snow, and wild animals running around in freezing places," I add.

I am thinking of "To Lie Down Lean," from her collection entitled *Never Trust a Crow*:

> Like the fox in his burrow
> I pull my walls around me, hoarding
> what light, what salvaged warmth
> glow inside.

Or this:

> She is a white bear in a white cave
> formed of a white world, lost in her own
> snow-colored dream.

"Is it always Wisconsin in your poems?" I ask.

"Sometimes," she answers. "I like to imagine what it must have been like in really isolated places, those cold and isolated houses and farms.

"But I like winter," she says. "I always have. All those years when I couldn't write, I kept thinking about a time when I could get snowed in for a whole winter, maybe on an island where no one could find me, and have a fire and music and do what I wanted and be *away*. From everyone."

"Including your husband?" I ask.

"*Especially* my husband," Lois confirms.

"Did you ever find your island?"

"By the time I could go, I didn't need it any more," Lois decides. "All it meant was getting the time I never had, and I have that now. This town is full of writers and artists, you know. I belong to four different writers' groups. My children call it my social life," she says proudly.

"You were never lonely?"

"I was lonely for years," she says. "It was a theme. Even around people.

But now I am not lonely, I am alone, and alone is no longer something that I dread."

I like to picture Lois Hayna in her office at home, which is packed with books and papers, reveling in being alone—and deconstructing fairy tales. I think of "Postscript," her Cinderella poem:

> I set it up, of course I set it up. Wishing
> gets a girl nowhere. I flattered him,
> teased him, and ran, leaving the slipper
> to point him to me. Charmed by his cleverness,
> he made me Queen.

Cinderella's manipulation leaves her unfulfilled and miserable at the poem's end, but that is not the part I think of. I prefer to imagine Lois, unencumbered by Prince Charmings, and perhaps with a pot of rosemary growing nearby, putting the story however she wants.

"You still garden," I say. "Why?"

She answers immediately. "It's such a miraculous thing, these perfect, scented, little leaves. But you know that."

"Maybe," I say. "What I like is digging big holes and making dirt."

"You," she laughs. "You're still in the mud pie phase. Trying to be absolutely elemental."

"Right," I say, laughing back.

That night I huddle under a thick down blanket. Fingers of wind creep in through every crack in the bedroom window frames. I finally fall asleep with a runny nose and wake up cranky, talking to myself, as I walk downstairs in heavy socks and a bathrobe, about having to learn how to install storm windows. My dog shoots past me, jumping and twisting to be let out.

"Okay," I say, "okay."

I open the front door, she runs ahead of me, I take three steps down to retrieve the newspaper and—chinook! A springlike wind has blown in and set about arranging a thaw. Already, the eaves are dripping.

I sit down and wait for the sun to move into position exactly where I like it, on my face and shoulders. The gentle wind feels like fingers in my hair. It blows in the smell of leaves decaying, however slowly, on top of dirt. I take my trowel in my hand, move the leaves aside, and scratch in the crumbling, thawing dirt, until I see the white of a spring bulb. A crocus, maybe? Then I cover it all back up.

The mud pie stage, Lois says. Elemental. Is it elemental to cleave to dirt because it gives you a place to put your feet? Something to smell? Or because, no matter what you have or don't have, you still have dirt?

At this appropriate moment, my dog, who has been rolling in a particularly potent mud slick, comes running back up the path to shake a fine spattering over me, my bathrobe, and my newspaper. Enough introspection, I tell myself. It is winter, but so what. Underneath the mounds of snow and leaves, there is dirt. Underneath all this, we are alive.

Acknowledgments

Grateful acknowledgment is made for permission to reprint poetry excerpts as follows:

Page 94: Howard Nemerov, "The Statues in the Public Garden" from *Mirrors and Images: Poems*, copyright© 1958, 1986, Howard Nemerov. Reprinted by permission of Margaret Nemerov.

Page 105: William Carlos Williams, "The Ivy Crown" from *Collected Poems 1939–1962: Volume II*, copyright© 1944, 1948, William Carlos Williams. Reprinted by permission of New Directions Publishing Corporation.

Page 117: Pablo Neruda, "Oda al Tomate" from *Odes to Common Things*. Spanish copyright© by Pablo Neruda and Fundación Pablo Neruda. English translation copyright© 1994 by Ken Krabbenhoft. Reprinted by permission of Little, Brown and Company.

Page 187: Lois Beebe Hayna, "Seeds as They Fall" from *Never Trust a Crow*, copyright© 1990, Lois Beebe Hayna. Reprinted by permission of James Andrews and Company, Golden, Colorado.